P9-DMQ-089

IN WILDNESS . . .

FROM Henry David Thoreau

"In Wildness Is the

INTRODUCTION BY Joseph Wood Krutch

Preservation of the World"

SELECTIONS & PHOTOGRAPHS BY

ELIOT PORTER

SIERRA CLUB ◆ SAN FRANCISCO

The Walden quotations conform with the Riverside Press edition of 1894. The Journal quotations, with one exception, conform with the *Journal* edition of 1906. The first autumn page, dated November 1, 1853, conforms to the Riverside edition, 1892. The poem in the autumn section comes from *A Week on the Concord and Merrimack Rivers.* The title comes from the essay entitled "Walking." The passages from Thoreau's Journal are published through the courtesy of Houghton Mifflin Co. The two opening lines of the Foreword are from "The Tuft of Flowers," by Robert Frost, copyright 1934 by Holt, Rinehart and Winston, Inc., copyright renewed 1962 by Robert Frost. They are reprinted by permission of Holt, Rinehart and Winston, Inc.

Library of Congress Catalog Card No. 62-20527
Manufactured in the United States of America
Seventh Printing

To Aline, who first suggested it

and

to Ellen, who taught me

detachment toward nature

this book is affectionately dedicated

The West of which I speak is but another name for the Wild, and what I have been preparing to say is, that in Wildness is the preservation of the World. Every tree sends its fibers forth in search of the Wild. The cities import it at any price. Men plow and sail for it. From the forest and wilderness come the tonics and barks which brace mankind. . . .

FOREWORD

'Men work together,' I told him from the heart
'Whether they work together or apart.'
—Robert Frost

Even to leaf through what has been created here is rewarding; but something quite wonderful happens to those who let themselves drift through. This is symbiotic art: Eliot Porter corroborates Thoreau and Thoreau verifies Porter, one never diminishing the other, for reasons Joseph Wood Krutch singles out as he tells how closely these men traveled together a century apart. Just as there is always something new to discover in Thoreau, there is much more than meets the eye in the photographs; a few impressions about the artist—the man who, ten years out of Harvard Medical School, gave up medicine and science for photography in 1939—may speed the discovery.

We ourselves discovered, or think we did, that the patience Dr. Porter acquired for bird photography has contributed enormously to the excellence of what he does here with inanimate subjects. He has learned to be alert to what a particular bird is likely to do in the next few minutes and to be ready when the bird meets his expectations. Having mastered the flightiness of such subjects, he could expect little trouble from the dependable peregrinations of sun, wind, and cloud.

The seasons performed just as dependably. Knowing a wild place well, Porter could anticipate what new life and form and color each change in the weather would reveal in that place, even as Thoreau had, and be there at the appointed hour. He would arrive fully sensitized and in sharp focus himself. Lens and image, we can see, responded unfailingly. If need be, abstractions would organize where only reality had been before. None but a very literal person would fail to see that color is his music, that there is melody line, counterpoint, harmony, dynamics, voicing, and phrasing all there for those who will listen.

There is absolute pitch, too—absolute color pitch. As we looked at the dye-transfer prints in Porter's exhibit, The Seasons, which the Smithsonian Institution circulates and from which the book derives, then peered at his four-by-five transparencies, and finally as we watched him review color proofs at the Barnes Press, we were quietly amazed by what this man knows about color. He remembers exactly what was there when the shutter let a moment's light in, and he knows what must happen technically if that moment is to be fixed. We have not yet seen all his colors in their natural habitat. But we are confident that if we borrow his acuity and walk out into waldens here and there, we shall find those colors ourselves. If we are very fortunate, once in a while they may perform for us the quiet symphony that responds to his baton.

Others, who are of unquestioned competence in these matters, must pass final judgment on Eliot Porter's greatness as a photographer. Some already have. I myself know only that I never saw color mean more than he makes it mean, and that I shall not easily overlook it again. The two Porter albums—the prints and the selections from Thoreau that were the manuscript for this book—made me vow openly to see it published even if I had to take up a life of crime to get the funds for it. Happily, Belvedere Scientific Fund intervened and provided generous assistance. It took responsible imagination to see as far beyond the mere beauty of the manuscript as needed seeing. Imaginative philanthropy followed.

To me it seems that much of what Henry David Thoreau wrote, more than a century ago, was less timely in his day than it is in ours: we can now prove that the natural and civilized worlds must live together or perish separately. We hope that the attitude of Thoreau and Porter toward unspoiled countryside will be pervasive. For there is no science and no art of greater importance than that which teaches seeing, which builds sensitivity and respect for the natural world, a world that "has visibly been recreated in the night." A natural world thus cherished will always bring "mornings when men are new-born, men who have the seeds of life in them."

DAVID BROWER

Berkeley, California
August 11, 1962

PREFACE

In a sense this book began when my father bought an island in Maine nearly half a century ago. Summer after summer its white beaches, its dense, spruce forests, its sour, salty, sea smells came back to life after the long gray winter. On Great Spruce Head Island among sweet fern and bunchberry, bay and twin flower, I found the tonic of wildness. In Maine I first read *Walden,* finding it rather a chore; in Maine I also became a photographer, and the subjects I photographed were things, I like to believe now, Thoreau might have described.

Shortly following World War II I became seriously involved with Thoreau's work. Just when this occurred and under what circumstances I no longer remember, but it was about this time that my wife suggested I do a book on Thoreau. My photographs, she thought, were like his writing. Her remark took deep root in my mind although I did little about it at first except to reread *Walden* and to collect Thoreau's works. Intermittently, in no logical order, I read them and slowly began to find out what kind of a person Thoreau had been and what he had said about the outdoors. At first I thought only the descriptive passages were suitable for a book of photographs, but on reading other authors, among whom Aldo Leopold and Joseph Wood Krutch influenced me most, those passages in which he wrote about man's relation to nature became greater in importance to the book I envisioned.

Fitting our time well and giving pause to our thoughts is Thoreau's admonition and despairing cry: "Most men, it seems to me, do not care for nature and would sell their share in all her beauty for a given sum. Thank God men have not yet learned to fly so they can lay waste the sky as well as the earth." Lines like these could not be illustrated, but they made me realize that illustration was not all I wanted to do. I hoped to be able to complement in feeling and spirit Thoreau's thinking one hundred years ago, and to show the peril we face even more today by our ever faster destruction of life not our own.

In the course of this time I was in Tucson one spring and with some hesitation went to Joseph Wood Krutch for advice on the book and to ask if he would write an introduction. To my surprise and delight he said he would. With this encouragement I went to work in earnest, selecting what I considered the best of Thoreau's writing, and photographing in all seasons the woods and streams and ponds and marshes in the northeastern states. Off and on for almost ten years this work continued until gradually text and photographs became part of one another. The time now seemed ripe to look for a publisher. I took it to several publishing houses and finally put it in the hands of an agent. It was rejected by all for the same reasons, their limited interest and its unlimited cost.

There was nothing I could do about the cost, but I could try to interest more people in the subject by making it more available. So I arranged an exhibition of prints and short quotations from Thoreau which I named "The Seasons." Following a first showing in Santa Fe, it went to Baltimore, Kansas City, and San Francisco; then the Smithsonian Institution asked for it as one of its traveling exhibitions. The first show under Smithsonian auspices was at George

Eastman House in Rochester, the opening of which I attended. While I was in Rochester Nancy Newhall introduced me by telephone to David Brower and suggested that the Sierra Club consider publishing the book. He asked to see it, was gratifyingly enthusiastic, and immediately set about obtaining the support necessary to make it a Sierra Club publication.

The title, a Thoreau quotation which the Wilderness Society has long used almost as a motto, was suggested by David Brower. Its eight words express the theme of the book and tell what Thoreau discovered one hundred years ago, that a leaven of wildness is necessary for the health of the human spirit, a truth we seem to have forgotten in our headlong rush to control all nature. Unless we reverse our course all wildness will disappear from the American continent even within the lives of those who are now the age Thoreau was when he died in 1862.

I wish to thank my wife Aline for her constant support, sympathy, and understanding during all the years that I worked on this book, Ellen Auerbach for her sensitive criticism and help with many of the pictures, Nancy Newhall for her work and encouragement in behalf of the book, Joseph Wood Krutch for his help and advice, directly and through his writings, in selecting many of the passages, and David Brower for his untiring devotion to highest publishing standards and to the purposes of the book.

ELIOT PORTER

Santa Fe, New Mexico
July 21, 1962

INTRODUCTION

Here, sensitively and with complete understanding, is presented through the medium of a new art that very world of American Nature which Thoreau, practicing one of the oldest of arts, taught us to see better than anyone ever had before. Eliot Porter makes no attempt merely to *document* the selected passages. To have done so would have been to produce no more than documentary illustrations. Instead—guided by sure artistic instinct—he has realized that the way to add to what Thoreau had written was to catch Thoreau's spirit, to see with his eye the kind of thing he saw and loved. As a result Porter's pictures are truly in the spirit of Thoreau.

What this means, first of all, is to discover how new and beautiful the familiar can be if we actually see it as though we had never seen it before. Other writers and other photographers are prone to seek out the unusual, the grandiose, and the far away. They shock us into awareness by flinging into our faces the obviously stupendous. When they are successful in their attempt they inspire in us that special sense of surprise, wonder, and a kind of pleasing terror which the eighteenth century defined as "awe." But the effect they produce is at the opposite pole from that aimed at and achieved by Thoreau.

John Muir is our great poet of the awesome aspects of the American scene. His subject matter complements that of Thoreau. But there could hardly be celebrants of nature more different. Thoreau's theme is not the remote and stupendous, but the daily and hourly miracle of the usually unnoticed beauty that is close at hand. He does not range the world seeking out the sensational. The chickadee and the violet are to him as striking as the flame tree or the bird of paradise. What we need is, he felt, not the unfamiliar but the power to realize that the familiar becomes unfamiliar once we really look at it, and that every aspect of the natural world is in its own way "awful."

One phase of the romantic revival of interest in nature was concerned especially with the "awesome" aspects. Byron illustrated this new interest when he wrote with a characteristically flamboyant rhetorical flourish his description of a thunderstorm in the Alps:

And this was in the night, Most glorious night
Thou wert not meant for slumber. Oh, let me be
A sharer in thy fierce and far delight,
A portion of the tempest and of thee.

Thoreau is far closer to Wordsworth and Wordsworth's even more familiar "The meanest flower that grows . . ." What one will find in Porter's pictures is the world of calm beauty at which one must look twice to find the awesomeness which is, nevertheless, there.

He with his camera—like Thoreau with his notebook and his "spyglass"—has "Traveled a good deal in Concord," and roundabout. The result is the very New England Thoreau saw more than one hundred years ago. Though the area still left to Nature has shrunk, what remains is what Thoreau saw, loved, and celebrated.

Even in his time he was aware that his beloved Concord had been more tamed than he would have liked to see it. "When I consider that the nobler animals have been exterminated here—the cougar, the panther, lynx, wolverine, wolf, bear, moose, the deer, the beaver, the turkey, etc., etc.—I cannot but feel as if I lived in a tame, and as it were, emasculated country. . . . I take infinite pains to know all the phenomena of spring, for instance, thinking that I have here the entire form, and then to my chagrin, I hear that it is but an imperfect copy that I possess and read, that my ancestors have torn out many of the first leaves and grandest passages, and mutilated it in many places." The process continues. Yet it may very well be that fewer animals and plants have actually disappeared completely since Thoreau's time than during the century that preceded him. It is the area left to them which has been most drastically curtailed. One must hunt longer to find what he found more readily. But as Porter's pictures show, most of the kind of thing he saw can still be seen.

How much longer that will be true is a question. Thoreau wondered that the village bell did not sound the knell when another tree was cut down. The trees continue to fall and any bell which is rung is less likely to be a knell than a celebration of Progress. "The squirrel has leaped to another tree, the hawk has circled further off, and is settled now upon a new eyrie, but the woodman is preparing to lay his axe at the root of that also."

So much for the subject matter of Porter's pictures. In what sense do their spirit and intention correspond to that of Thoreau?

Photography is the most modern but at the same time the least "modernistic" of the arts. Proponents of abstraction, surrealism, and the rest have long been accustomed to say that the camera has relieved the painter of a former function, namely, that of representation. Whether or not to be so relieved is actually a boon is still open to question. But there is no doubt about the fact that the photographer does deal in representations of the actual, whether it be the actuality of an external Nature or the actuality of a human portrait. Yet it is very far from true that he need be merely mechanical, that he can have no personal vision. He cannot, like the painter, impose upon Nature a pattern or design which isn't there. But he can select and frame his picture in such a way as to reveal the pattern and design which the merely casual observer has failed to see, either because he did not look closely enough or because it was confused by adjacent irrelevancies. The more the painter invents, the farther he takes us from the world which actually exists and to that extent he may even encourage us in an alienation from the real. The master photographer, on the other hand, discovers rather than invents, and in that way he may (as Porter so strikingly does) second Thoreau in Thoreau's most insistent injunction, namely, "Be not among those who have eyes that see not and ears that hear not."

It was no small task to select from the twenty volumes of Thoreau's published writings passages both so interesting in themselves and so susceptible to supplement and illumination by companion photographs as are those Porter has presented. Comparatively few of even those who profess an admiration for Thoreau's spirit have read one-tenth of what he left behind in the Journal from which he quarried his major published works, and from which he might have drawn several others. Many of his most brilliant passages of description and comment are buried in a text much of which became more pedestrian as the years went by. But Porter has ranged through the whole corpus and selected with so sure an insight those passages which are both remarkable in themselves and most suitable for his special undertaking that this volume is, among other things, one of the best anthologies ever compiled. His book is something to be read as well as looked at, and there is no student of his author so well versed that he will not get new insights from it.

Admirers of Walden and of the enormously rich Journal have found in them many different things: a theory of economics, a defense of nonconformity, a definition of the good life, and a defense of Thoreau's most persistent contention, namely, that human existence should be, not a duty or a burden, not a mere means to an end, but a self-justifying esthetic joy. Puritan in certain respects he was, but in this last mentioned attitude he was among the most defiant of antipuritans, as when he proclaimed that God had not sent him into this world without some spending money.

With none of these aspects of Thoreau's philosophy is Porter concerned, except perhaps by inference. What he does, however, illustrate so vividly is the conviction which underlies all the others, namely, the conviction that the source of the joy he sought, and of the wisdom he hoped to acquire, as well as the justification for his neglect of what others called the serious business of life, is the fact that "this curious world which we inhabit is more wonderful than it is convenient; more beautiful than it is useful; it is more to be admired and enjoyed than used."

Emanuel Kant propounded the theory that the magic of art depends in large part upon the various means which it uses to isolate the thing represented from all ordinary desires and duties in such a way that the only reaction possible to it is pure contemplation. We cannot pick the painted flower nor embrace the woman whom the artist has placed upon canvas. We can only look, see, and realize them. It was thus that Thoreau wished to contemplate rather than use Nature, and it is thus that we can enjoy Porter's photographs.

This is by no means to say that Thoreau was a mere esthete, one that is to whom natural beauty means only line, and shape, and color. In fact, some of the most heartfelt expressions of the scorn he was capable of is directed against those who, like the once popular English analyst of the picturesque William Gilpin, saw in Nature nothing except a picture. Gilpin talked, he said, "as if there were some food for the soul in mere light and shadow." He had, for example, undertaken to explain how a sleek well-fed horse might, no less than a shaggy one, be picturesque. "It is not his smooth and shining coat that makes him so. It is the apparent interruption of that smoothness by a variety of shades, and colors, which produces the effect." And Thoreau comments thus: "Not the slightest reference to the fact that this surface, with its lights and shades, belongs to a horse and not to a bag of wind. The same reasoning would apply equally well to one of his hind quarters hung bottom upwards in a butcher's stall. . . . I should say that no arrangement of light and shadow without reference to the object, actual or suggested, so lit and shaded can interest us powerfully, any more than paint itself can charm us." Gilpin had no fellow feeling, no sense of warmness.

Moreover, if Thoreau was no esthete, he was, if anything, still less a scientist—in the driest meaning of that term. It enraged him to buy a book on turtles and to find it nothing but anatomy. He did not, he protested, care to know the length of a hen hawk's intestines. And he had a deep sense of guilt when he once consented to send to Agassiz for pickling a specimen from his beloved Walden pond. If Nature was not a mere abstraction—as he feared it was to neighbor Emerson—neither was it something to be learned *about* rather than something to be learned from. On the one hand "it is not worthwhile to go around the world to count the cats in Zanzibar;" on the other, "a man has not seen a thing until he has felt it." One cannot even begin to "love Nature" in any profitable sense until one has achieved an empathy, a sense of oneness and of participation. "Appreciation" means an identification, a sort of mystical experience, religious in the most fundamental sense of the terms.

If the modern world is to learn from him what he has to teach, it must try to understand the what, why, and wherefore of the life he led and of his conviction that the only good life possible is one "natural" in a sense that society has tended more and more to corrupt. What, one must still ask, does it mean to observe Nature, to live with Nature, and to learn from it? How does one go about doing any of these things and what is it that one may hope to learn?

The two themes which reappear so persistently seem at first sight strangely disparate. On the one hand was Thoreau's search for what he called "wildness"; on the other, the search for the "higher laws" he never more than glimpsed but which he was sure Nature, even in her most savage aspects, was persistently whispering to him. The one search seems atavistic, the other transcendental, as though he were both going back to savagery and forward toward some higher mystical state. But the paradox is not unresolvable and in the resolution is the core of his faith.

Wildness, the merely natural and therefore almost animal life, is not sought for its own sake. Thoreau was no mere romantic admirer of the noble savage, and in Walden itself he makes this plain by examining the deficiencies of the best natural man he had ever known, namely the woodchopper. But the human race has lost its way. The road upward from the savage does not lead to the cluttered, materialistic, and desperate life such as that he sees his neighbors leading. To find the right road one must return in reality as well as in imagination to the origins. From them one might go forward again to a truly civilized, not a merely artificial, way of life.

Thoreau was aware that of his program he had achieved anything like full success only in what might be called its preliminary phases. He had simplified his life to the point where he had around it the wide margin which permitted him to live, rather than merely to make a living. He had made himself an inspector of snowstorms, and he had observed many natural phenomena. Certainly also he had achieved empathy—with both the wildness and the gentleness of Nature. Because of these successes he was sufficiently sure that he was on the right road confidently to advise others to take it. He had learned that it is not necessary to live by the sweat of one's brow unless "you sweat more easily than I do." He had found a happiness and contentment which were to him sure proof that his way of life was approved by whatever gods may be. But of the higher laws he admitted that he had caught only whispered hints. That chapter of Walden called "Higher Laws" merely reaffirms his sympathy with wildness along with his feeling that we have only begun to transcend it. No full revelation comes. But in the last chapter he can make the confident proclamation that "there is more day to dawn."

Just one hundred years ago Thoreau died. Before his death he shocked a pious relative who had asked if he had made his peace with God, by replying, "I am not aware that we ever quarreled." In the century which has passed since then no one has gone further than he along the road he chose and most have turned their backs even more irrevocably upon it. And whether or not this is the reason, the fact remains that the mass of men lead lives of a less and less quiet desperation. If those who believe in progress and define it as they do continue to have their way it will soon be impossible either to test his theory that Nature is the only proper context of human life or that in such a context we may ultimately learn the "higher laws."

One important function of a book like this will have been performed if it persuades those who open it that some remnant of the beauties it calls to our attention is worth preserving.

JOSEPH WOOD KRUTCH

Tucson, Arizona
June 14, 1962

FROM Henry David Thoreau

SELECTIONS AND PHOTOGRAPHS BY Eliot Porter

SPRING

Remember thy creator in the days of thy youth. Rise free from care before the dawn, and seek adventures. Let the noon find thee by other lakes, and the night overtake thee everywhere at home. There are no larger fields than these, no worthier games than may here be played. Grow wild according to thy nature, like these sedges and brakes, which will never become English hay. Let the thunder rumble; what if it threaten ruin to farmers' crops? That is not its errand to thee. Take shelter under the cloud, while they flee to carts and sheds. Let not to get a living be thy trade, but thy sport. Enjoy the land, but own it not. Through want of enterprize and faith men are where they are, buying and selling, and spending their lives like serfs. — *Walden*

February 12, 1860

At a distance in several directions I see the tawny earth streaked or spotted with white where the bank or hills and fields appear, or else the green-black evergreen forests, or the brown, or russet, or tawny deciduous woods, and here and there, where the agitated surface of the river is exposed, the blue-black water. That dark-eyed water, especially where I see it at right angles with the direction of the sun, is it not the first sign of spring? How its darkness contrasts with the general lightness of the winter! It has more life in it than any part of the earth's surface. It is where one of the arteries of the earth is palpable, visible.

March 8, 1840

In the brooks the slight grating sound of small cakes of ice, floating with various speed, is full of content and promise, and where the water gurgles under a natural bridge, you may hear these hasty rafts hold conversation in an undertone. Every rill is a channel for the juices of the meadow. Last year's grasses and flower-stalks have been steeped in rain and snow, and now the brooks flow with meadow tea. . . .

March 10, 1859

These earliest spring days are peculiarly pleasant. We shall have
no more of them for a year. I am apt to forget that we may have raw and
blustering days a month hence. The combination of this delicious air,
which you do not want to be warmer or softer, with the presence
of ice and snow, you sitting on the bare russet portions, the south
hillsides, of the earth, this is the charm of these days. It is the
summer beginning to show itself like an old friend in the midst of winter.
You ramble from one drier russet patch to another. These are
your stages. You have the air and sun of summer, over snow
and ice, and in some places even the rustling of dry leaves
under your feet, as in Indian-summer days.

March 30, 1840

Pray, what things interest me at present? A long, soaking rain,
the drops trickling down the stubble, while I lay drenched on last year's
bed of wild oats, by the side of some bare hill, ruminating.
These things are of moment. To watch this crystal globe just sent
from heaven to associate with me. While these clouds and this sombre
drizzling weather shut all in, we two draw nearer and know one another.
The gathering in of the clouds with the last rush and dying breath
of the wind, and then the regular dripping of twigs and leaves the country
o'er, the impression of inward comfort and sociableness, the drenched
stubble and trees that drop beads on you as you pass, their dim outline
seen through the rain on all sides dropping in sympathy with yourself.
These are my undisputed territory. This is Nature's English comfort. The
birds draw closer and are more familiar under the thick foliage,
composing new strains on their roosts against the sunshine.

March 10, 1859

I perceive the spring in the softened air . . . Looking through
this transparent vapor, all surfaces, not osiers and open water alone,
look more vivid. The hardness of winter is relaxed.
There is a fine effluence surrounding the wood, as if the sap had begun
to stir and you could detect it a mile off. Such is the difference
between an object seen through a warm, moist, and soft air and a cold,
dry, hard one. Such is the genialness of nature that the trees appear to have
put out feelers by which the senses apprehend them more tenderly.
I do not know that the woods are ever more beautiful, or affect me more.

March 17, 1859

When I am opposite the end of the willow-row, seeing the osiers of
perhaps two years old all in a mess, they are seen to be very distinctly
yellowish beneath and scarlet above. They are fifty rods off.
Here is the same chemistry that colors the leaf or fruit, coloring the bark.
It is generally, perhaps always, the upper part of the twig, the more
recent growth, that is the higher-colored and more flower or fruit like.
So leaves are more ethereal the higher up and farther from the root.
In the bark of the twigs, indeed, is the more permanent flower
or fruit. The flower falls in spring or summer, the fruit and leaves fall or
wither in autumn, but the blushing twigs retain their color
throughout the winter and appear more brilliant than ever
the succeeding spring. They are winter fruit.

March 30, 1856

How silent are the footsteps of spring! There, too, where there is a fraction of the meadow, two rods over, quite bare, under the bank, in this warm recess at the head of the meadow, though the rest of the meadow is covered with snow a foot or more in depth, I was surprised to see the skunk-cabbage, with its great spear-heads open and ready to blossom . . . The spring advances in spite of snow and ice, and cold even.

December 24, 1841

I want to go soon and live away by the pond, where I shall hear only the wind whispering among the reeds. It will be success if I shall have left myself behind. But my friends ask what I will do when I get there. Will it not be employment enough to watch the progress of the seasons?

For the first week, whenever I look out on the pond it impressed me like a tarn high up on the side of a mountain, its bottom far above the surface of other lakes, and, as the sun rose, I saw it throwing off its nightly clothing of mist, and here and there, by degrees, its soft ripples or its smooth reflecting surface was revealed, while the mists, like ghosts, were stealthily withdrawing in every direction into the woods, as at the breaking up of some nocturnal conventicle. The very dew seemed to hang upon the trees later into the day than usual, as on the sides of mountains.

— *Walden*

April 9, 1859

We sit by the side of little Goose Pond . . . to watch the ripples on it.
Now it is merely smooth, and then there drops down on to it, deep as it
lies amid the hills, a sharp and narrow blast of the icy north wind
careening above, striking it, perhaps, by a point or an edge,
and swiftly spreading along it, making a dark-blue ripple. Now four or
five windy bolts, sharp or blunt, strike it at once and spread
different ways. The boisterous but playful north wind evidently stoops
from a considerable height to dally with this fair pool which it discerns
beneath. You could sit there and watch these blue shadows playing
over the surface like the light and shade on changeable silk, for hours.
It reminds me, too, of the swift Camilla on a field [of] grain.
The wind often touches the water only by the finest points or edges.
It is thus when you look in some measure from the sun, but if you move
around so as to come more opposite to him, then these dark-blue
ripples are all sparkles too bright to look at, for now you see
the sides of the wavelets which reflect the sun to you.

March 28, 1859

How charming the contrast of land and water, especially a temporary island in the flood, with its new and tender shores of waving outline, so withdrawn yet habitable, above all if it rises into a hill high above the water and contrasting with it the more, and if that hill is wooded, suggesting wilderness! Our vernal lakes have a beauty to my mind which they would not possess if they were more permanent. Everything is in rapid flux here, suggesting that Nature is alive to her extremities and superficies.

March 10, 1853

This is the first really spring day . . . Something analogous to the thawing of the ice seems to have taken place in the air. At the end of winter there is a season in which we are daily expecting spring, and finally a day when it arrives . . . Methinks the first obvious evidence of spring is the pushing out of the swamp willow catkins . . . then the pushing up of skunk-cabbage spathes (and pads at the bottom of water).

October 25, 1857

She appears, and we are once more children; we commence again our course with the new year.

March 18, 1858

Each new year is a surprise to us. We find that we had virtually forgotten the note of each bird, and when we hear it again it is remembered like a dream, reminding us of a previous state of existence. How happens it that the associations it awakens are always pleasing, never saddening; reminiscenses of our sanest hours? The voice of nature is always encouraging.

June 2, 1858

Probably these crests of the earth are for the most part of one color in all lands, that gray color . . . which nature loves; color of unpainted wood, weather-stain, time-stain; not glaring nor gaudy; the color of all roofs, the color of all things that endure, the color that wears well; color of Egyptians ruins, of mummies and all antiquity: baked in the sun, done brown . . . not scarlet, like the crest of the bragging cock, but that hard, enduring gray; a terrene sky-color; solidified air with a tinge of earth.

March 13, 1842

Nature doth thus kindly heal every wound. By the mediation of a thousand little mosses and fungi, the most unsightly objects become radiant of beauty. There seem to be two sides of this world, presented us at different times, as we see things in growth or dissolution, in life or death. For seen with the eye of the poet, as God sees them, all things are alive and beautiful; but seen with the historical eye, or eye of the memory, they are dead and offensive. If we see Nature as pausing, immediately all mortifies and decays; but seen as progressing, she is beautiful.

May 23, 1853

How different the ramrod jingle of the chewink or any bird's note
sounds now at 5 P.M. in the cooler, stiller air, when also the humming of
insects is more distinctly heard, and perchance some impurity has
begun to sink to earth strained by the air! Or is it, perchance,
to be referred to the cooler, more clarified and pensive state of the mind,
when dews have begun to descend in it and clarify it? Chaste eve!
A certain lateness in the sound, pleasing to hear, which releases me
from the obligation to return in any particular season. I have passed the
Rubicon of staying out. I have said to myself, that way is not homeward;
I will wander further from what I have called my home—to the
home which is forever inviting me. In such an hour the freedom
of the woods is offered me, and the birds sing my dispensation.
In dreams the links of life are united: we forget that
our friends are dead; we know them as of old.

March 18, 1858

But, ah! the needles of the pine, how they shine, as I look down
over the Holden wood and westward! Every tree is lit with the most
subdued, but clear ethereal light, as if it were the most delicate frost work
in a winter morning, reflecting no heat, but only light.
And as they rock and wave in the strong wind, even a mile off,
the light courses up and down there as over a field of grain; . . . like
looms above the forest, when the shuttle is thrown between
the light woof and the dark web. . . .

February 25, 1860

I noticed yesterday the first conspicuous silvery sheen from the needles
of the white pine waving in the wind. A small one was conspicuous by the
side of the road. . . . I suspect that those plumes which
have been oppressed or contracted by snow and ice are not only dried
but opened and spread by the wind.

March 10, 1852

I was reminded, this morning before I rose, of those undescribed ambrosial mornings of summer which I can remember, when a thousand birds were heard gently twittering and ushering in the light, like the argument to a new canto of an epic and heroic poem. The serenity, the infinite promise, of such a morning! The song or twitter of birds drips from the leaves like dew. Then there was something divine and immortal in our life, when I have waked up on my couch in the woods and seen the day dawning, and heard the twittering of the birds.

Early in May, the oaks, hickories, maples, and other trees, just putting out amidst the pine woods around the pond, imparted a brightness like sunshine to the landscape, especially in cloudy days, as if the sun were breaking through mists and shining faintly on the hill-sides here and there. — *Walden*

June 1, 1854

Within a little more than a fortnight the woods, from bare twigs, have become a sea of verdure, and young shoots have contended with one another in the race. The leaves are unfurled all over the country. . . . Shade is produced, and the birds are concealed and their economies go forward uninterruptedly, and a covert is afforded to animals generally. But thousands of worms and insects are preying on the leaves while they are young and tender. Myriads of little parasols are suddenly spread all the country over, to shield the earth and the roots of the trees from the parching heat, and they begin to flutter and rustle in the breeze.

May 9, 1852

It is impossible to remember a week ago. A river of Lethe flows
with many windings the year through, separating one season from another.
The heavens for a few days have been lost. It has been a sort of
paradise instead. As with the seashore, so it is with the universal
earth-shore, not in summer can you look far into the ocean
of the ether. They who come to this world as to a watering-place in the
summer for coolness and luxury never get the far and fine
November views of heaven. Is not all the summer akin to a paradise?
We have to bathe in ponds to brace ourselves. The earth is
blue now,—the near hills, in this haze.

September 28, 1852

Ah, if I could put into words that music which I hear; that music which can bring tears to the eyes of marble statues!—to which the very muscles of men are obedient!

May 17, 1854

The splendid rhodora now sets the swamps on fire with its masses of rich color. It is *one of the first* flowers to catch the eye at a distance in masses,—so naked, unconcealed by its own leaves.

May 23, 1854

We soon get through with Nature. She excites an expectation which she cannot satisfy. The merest child which has rambled into a copsewood dreams of a wildness so wild and strange and inexhaustible as Nature can never show him. . . . There was a time when the beauty and the music were all within, and I sat and listened to my thoughts, and there was a song in them. I sat for hours on rocks and wrestled with the melody which possessed me. I sat and listened by the hour to a positive though faint and distant music, not sung by any bird, nor vibrating any earthly harp. When you walked with a joy which knew not its own origin. When you were an organ of which the world was but one poor broken pipe. I lay long on the rocks, foundered like a harp on the seashore, that knows not how it is dealt with. You sat on the earth as on a raft, listening to music that was not of the earth, but which ruled and arranged it. Man *should be* the harp articulate. When you cords were tense.

March 22, 1861

When we consider how soon some plants which spread rapidly,
by seeds or roots, would cover an area equal to the surface of the globe,
. . . how soon some fishes would fill the ocean if all their ova
became full-grown fishes, we are tempted to say that every organism,
whether animal or vegetable, is contending for the possession of the
planet. . . . Nature opposes to this many obstacles, as climate, myriads of
brute and also human foes, and of competitors which may preoccupy
the ground. Each suggests an immense and wonderful greediness
and tenacity of life . . . as if bent on taking entire possession of the globe
wherever the climate and soil will permit. And each prevails
as much as it does, because of the ample preparations it has made
for the contest, — it has secured a myriad chances, — because
it never depends on spontaneous generation to save it.

March 23, 1856

I seek acquaintance with Nature, — to know her moods and manners.
Primitive nature is the most interesting to me. I take infinite pains to
know all the phenomena of spring, for instance, thinking that I have here
the entire poem, and then, to my chagrin, I learn that it is but
an imperfect copy that I possess and have read, that my ancestors have
torn out many of the first leaves and grandest passages, and mutilated it
in many places. I should not like to think that some demigod
had come before me and picked out some of the best of the stars.
I wish to know an entire heaven and an entire earth.

SUMMER

We need the tonic of wildness, to wade sometimes in marshes where the bittern and the meadow-hen lurk, and hear the booming of the snipe; to smell the whispering sedge where only some wilder and more solitary fowl builds her nest, and the mink crawls with its belly close to the ground. At the same time that we are earnest to explore and learn all things, we require that all things be mysterious and unexplorable, that land and sea be infinitely wild, unsurveyed and unfathomed by us because unfathomable. We can never have enough of nature. We must be refreshed by the sight of inexhaustible vigor, vast and titanic features, the sea-coast with its wrecks, the wilderness with its living and its decaying trees, the thunder cloud, and the rain which lasts three weeks and produces freshets. We need to witness our own limits transgressed, and some life pasturing freely where we never wander. — *Walden*

I am a parcel of vain strivings tied
By a chance bond together,
Dangling this way and that, their links
Were made so loose and wide,
Methinks,
For milder weather.

A bunch of violets without their roots,
And sorrel intermixed,
Encircled by a wisp of straw
Once coiled about their shoots,
The law
By which I'm fixed.

A nosegay which Time clutched from out
Those fair Elysian fields,
With weeds and broken stems, in haste,
Doth make the rabble rout
That waste
The day he yields.

And here I bloom for a short hour unseen,
Drinking my juices up,
With no root in the land
To keep my branches green,
But stand
In a bare cup.

Some tender buds were left upon my stem
In mimicry of life,
But ah! the children will not know,
Till time has withered them,
The woe
With which they're rife.

But now I see I was not plucked for naught,
And after in life's vase
Of glass set while I might survive,
But by a kind hand brought
Alive
To a strange place.

That stock thus thinned will soon redeem its hours,
And by another year,
Such as God knows, with freer air,
More fruits and fairer flowers
Will bear,
While I droop here.

June 6, 1856

How well suited the lining of a bird's nest, not only for the comfort of the young, but to keep the eggs from breaking! Fine elastic grass stems or root fibers, pine needles, or hair, or the like. These tender and brittle things which you can hardly carry in cotton lie there without harm.

June 6, 1857

This is June, the month of grass and leaves. . . . Already the aspens are trembling again, and a new summer is offered me. I feel a little fluttered in my thoughts, as if I might be too late. Each season is but an infinitesimal point. It no sooner comes than it is gone. It has no duration. It simply gives a tone and hue to my thought. Each annual phenomenon is a reminiscence and prompting. Our thoughts and sentiments answer to the revolutions of the seasons, as two cog-wheels fit into each other. We are conversant with only one point of contact at a time, from which we receive a prompting and impulse and instantly pass to a new season or point of contact. A year is made up of a certain series and number of sensations and thoughts which have their language in nature. Now I am ice, now I am sorrel. Each experience reduces itself to a mood of the mind.

June 11, 1852

As I climbed the Cliffs, when I jarred the foliage, I perceived an exquisite perfume which I could not trace to its source. Ah, those fugacious universal fragrances of the meadows and woods! odors rightly mingled!

June 14, 1851

Where my path crosses the brook in the meadow there is a singularly sweet scent in the heavy air . . . where the brakes grow,—the fragrance of the earth, as if the dew were a distillation of the fragrant essences of Nature. . . . And now my senses are captivated again by a sweet fragrance as I enter the embowered willow causeway, and I know not if it be from a particular plant or all together,—
sweet-scented vernal grass or sweet-brier.

June 9, 1850

Who taught the oven-bird to conceal her nest? It is on the ground, yet out of sight. What cunning there is in nature! No man could have arranged it more artfully for the purpose of concealment. Only the escape of the bird betrays it.

July 3, 1853

The Oven-bird's nest in Laurel Glen is near the edge of an open pine wood, under a fallen pine twig and a heap of dry oak leaves. Within these, on the ground, is the nest, with a dome-like top and an arched entrance of the whole height and width on one side. Lined within with dry pine needles.

June 7, 1853

The oven-bird runs from her covered nest, so close to the ground under the lowest twigs and leaves, even the loose leaves on the ground, like a mouse, that I cannot get a fair view of her. She does not fly at all. Is it to attract me, or partly to protect herself?

June 26, 1852

And the water-lily floats on the smooth surface of slow waters, amid rounded shields of leaves, bucklers, red beneath, which simulate a green field, perfuming the air. Each instantly the prey of the spoiler,— the rose-bug and water-insects. How transitory the perfect beauty of the rose and the lily! The highest, intensest color belongs to the land, the purest, perchance, to the water. The lily is perhaps the only flower which all are eager to pluck. . . .

June 20, 1853

Found two lilies open in the very shallow inlet of the meadow. Exquisitely beautiful, and unlike anything else that we have, is the first white lily just expanded in some shallow lagoon where the water is leaving it,—perfectly fresh and pure, before the insects have discovered it. How admirable its purity! How innocently sweet its fragrance! How significant that the rich, black mud of our dead stream produces the water-lily,—out of that fertile slime springs this spotless purity! It is remarkable that those flowers which are most emblematical of purity should grow in the mud.

July 4, 1860

Standing on J. P. Brown's land, south side, I observed his rich and luxuriant uncut grass-lands northward, now waving under the easterly wind. It is a beautiful camilla, sweeping like waves of light and shade over the whole breadth of his land, like a low steam curling over it, imparting wonderful life to the landscape, like the light and shade of a changeable garment. . . . It is an interesting feature, very easily overlooked, and suggests that we are wading and navigating at present in a sort of sea of grass, which yields and undulates under the wind like water; and so, perchance, the forest is seen to do from a favorable position.

Early, there was that flashing light of waving pine in the horizon; now, the Camilla on grass and grain.

June 30, 1840

In this fresh evening each blade and leaf looks as if it had been dipped in an icy liquid greenness.

June 4, 1854

Now is the time [to] observe the leaves, so fair in color and so perfect on form. I stood over a sprig of choke-cherry, with fair and perfect glossy green obovate and serrate leaves, in the woods this P.M., as if it were a rare flower. Now the various forms of oak leaves in the sprout-lands, wet-glossy, as if newly painted green and varnished, attract me. The chinquapin and black shrub oaks are such leaves as I fancy crowns were made of. And in the washing breeze the lighter undersides begin to show, and a new light is flashed upon the year, lighting up and enlivening the landscape.

June 22, 1853

As I come over the hill, I hear the wood thrush singing his evening lay.
This is the only bird whose note affects me like music, affects the flow
and tenor of my thoughts, my fancy and imagination. It lifts and
exhilerates me. . . . It is a medicative draught to my soul.
It is an elixir to my eyes and a fountain of youth to all my senses.
It changes all hours to an eternal morning. It banishes all trivialness.
It reinstates me in my dominion, makes me the lord of creation, is chief
musician of my court. This minstrel sings in a time, a heroic age, with
which no event in the village can be contemporary. How can they be
contemporary when only the latter is *temporary* at all? . . . So there is
something in the music of the cow-bell, something sweeter and
more nutritious, than in the milk which the farmers drink. This thrush's
song is a *ranz des vaches* to me. I long for wildness, a nature which
I cannot put my foot through, woods where the woodthrush forever sings,
where the hours are early morning ones, and there is dew on the grass,
and the day is forever unproved, where I might have a fertile
unknown for a soil about me. I would go after the cows,
I would watch the flocks of Admetus there forever, only for my board
and clothes, a New Hampshire everlasting and unfallen. . . .
All that was ripest and fairest in the wildness and the wild man is
preserved and transmitted to us in the strain of the wood thrush. It is the
mediator between barbarism and civilization. It is unrepentant as Greece.

June 27, 1859

I find an *Attacus luna* half hidden under a skunk-cabbage leaf,
with its back to the ground and motionless, on the edge of a swamp.
The under side is a particularly pale hoary green. It is somewhat greener
above with a slightly purplish brown border on the front edge of its
front wings, and a brown, yellow, and whitish eye-spot in the middle of
each wing. It is very sluggish and allows me to turn it over
and cover it up with another leaf, — sleeping till the night comes.
It has more relation to the moon by its pale hoary-green color and its
sluggishness by day than by the form of its tail.

June 23, 1852

It seems natural that rocks which have lain under the heavens so long should be gray, as it were an intermediate color between the heavens and the earth. The air is the thin paint in which they have been dipped and brushed with the wind. Water, which is more fluid and like the sky in its nature, is still more like it in color. Time will make the most discordant materials harmonize. . . .

June 17, 1854

A cold fog. These mornings those who walk in grass are thoroughly wetted above mid-leg. All the earth is dripping wet. I am surprised to feel how warm the water is, by contrast with the cold, foggy air. . . .
The dewy cobwebs are very thick this morning, little napkins of the fairies spread on the grass.

July 7, 1852

There is everywhere dew on the cobwebs, little gossamer veils or scarfs as big as your hand, dropped from the fairy shoulders that danced on the grass the past night.

November 9, 1857

Mr. Farmer tells me that one Sunday he went to his barn, having
nothing to do, and thought he would watch the swallows, republican
swallows. The old bird was feeding her young, and he sat within
fifteen feet, overlooking them. There were five young, and he was curious
to know how each received its share; and as often as the bird came
with a fly, the one at the door (or opening) took it, and then they all
hitched round one notch, so that a new one was presented at the door,
who received the next fly; and this was the invariable order, the
same one never received two flies in succession. At last the old bird
brought a very small fly, and the young one that swallowed it did not
desert his ground but waited to receive the next, but when
the bird came with another, of the usual size, she commenced a loud
and long scolding at the little one, till it resigned its place,
and the next in succession received the fly.

The large buds, suddenly pushing out late in the spring from dry sticks which had seemed to be dead, developed themselves as by magic into graceful green and tender boughs, an inch in diameter; and sometimes as I sat at my window, so heedlessly did they grow and tax their weak joints, I heard a fresh and tender bough suddenly fall like a fan to the ground, when there was not a breath of air stirring, broken off by its own weight. In August, the large masses of berries, which, when in flower, had attracted many wild bees, gradually assumed their bright velvety crimson hue, and by their weight again bent down and broke the tender limbs. — *Walden*

October 26, 1853

I well remember the time this year when I first heard the dream of the toads. I was laying out house-lots on Little River in Haverhill. We had had some raw, cold and wet weather. But this day was remarkably warm and pleasant, and I had thrown off my outside coat. I was going home to dinner, past a shallow pool, which was green with springing grass, . . . when it occurred to me that I heard the dream of the toad. It rang through and filled all the air, though I had not heard it once. And I turned my companion's attention to it, but he did not appear to perceive it as a new sound in the air. Loud and prevailing as it is, most men do not notice it at all. It is to them, perchance, a sort of simmering or seething of all nature. That afternoon the dream of the toads rang through the elms by Little River and affected the thoughts of men, though they were not conscious that they heard it. How watchful we must be to keep the crystal well that we are made, clear!

June 17, 1854

It is dry, hazy June weather. We are more of the earth, farther from
heaven these days. We live in a grosser element. We [are] getting deeper
into the mists of earth. Even the birds sing with less vigor and
vivacity. The season of hope and promise is past; already the season
of small fruits has arrived. The Indian marked the midsummer as the
season when berries were ripe. We are a little saddened,
because we begin to see the interval between our hopes and their
fulfillment. The prospect of the heavens is taken way,
and we are presented only with a few small berries.

June 25, 1858

Sitting on the Conantum house sill (still left), I see two and perhaps three young striped squirrels, two-thirds grown, within fifteen or twenty feet, one or more on the wall and another on the ground.
Their tails are rather imperfect, as their bodies. They are running about, yet rather feebly, nibbling the grass, etc., or sitting upright, looking very cunning. The broad white line above and below the eye make it look very long as well as large, and the black and white stripe on its sides, curved as it sits, are very conspicuous and pretty. Who striped
the squirrel's side? Several times I saw two approach each other and playfully and, as it were, affectionatly put their paws and noses to each other's faces. Yet this was done very deliberately and affectionately. There was no rudeness nor excessive activity in the sport. At length the old one appears, larger and much more bluish, and shy, and,
with a sharp cluck or chip, calls the others gradually to her and draws them off along the wall, they from time to time frisking ahead
of her, then she ahead of them. The hawks must get many
of these inexperienced creatures.

AUTUMN

November 1, 1853

Few come to the woods to see how the pine lives and grows and spires, lifting its evergreen arms to the light, to see its perfect success. Most are content to behold it in the shape of many broad boards brought to market, and deem that its true success. The pine is no more lumber than man is, and to be made into boards and houses is no more its true and highest use than the truest use of man is to be cut down and made into manure. A pine cut down, a dead pine, is no more a pine than a dead human carcass is a man. Is it the lumberman who is the friend and lover of the pine, stands nearest to it, and understands its nature best? Is it the tanner or turpentine distiller who posterity will fable was changed into a pine at last? No, no, it is the poet who makes the truest use of the pine, who does not fondle it with an axe, or tickle it with a saw, or stroke it with a plane. It is the poet who loves it as his own shadow in the air, and lets it stand. It is as immortal as I am, and will go to as high a heaven, there to tower above me still. Can he who has only discovered the value of whale-bone and whale-oil be said to have discovered the true uses of the whale? Can he who slays the elephant for his ivory be said to have seen the elephant? No, these are petty and accidental uses. Just as if a stronger race were to kill us in order to make buttons and flageolets of our bones, and then prate of the usefulness of man. Every creature is better alive than dead, both men and moose and pine-trees, as life is more beautiful than death.

Flint's Pond! Such is the poverty of our nomenclature. What right had the unclean and stupid farmer, whose farm abutted on this sky water, whose shores he had ruthlessly laid bare, to give his name to it? Some skin-flint, who loved better the reflecting surface of a dollar, or a bright cent, in which he could see his own brazen face; who regarded even the wild ducks which settled in it as trespassers; his fingers grown into crooked and horny talons from the long habit of grasping harpy-like;—so it is not named for me. I go not there to see him nor to hear of him; who never *saw* it, who never bathed in it, who never loved it, who never protected it, who never spoke a good word for it, nor thanked God that He made had it. Rather let it be named from the fishes that swim in it, the wild fowl or quadrupeds which frequent it, the wild flowers which grow by its shores, or some wild man or child the thread of whose history is interwoven with its own; not from him who could show no title to it but the deed which a like-minded neighbor or legislature gave him,—him who thought only of its money value; whose present perchance cursed all the shore; who exhausted the land around it, and would fain have exhausted the waters within it; who regretted only that it was not English hay or cranberry meadow,—there was nothing to redeem it, forsooth, in his eyes,—and would have drained and sold it for the mud at its bottom. It did not turn his mill, and it was no privilege to him to behold it. I respect not his labors, his farm where everything has its price, who would carry the landscape, who would carry his God, to market, if he could get anything for him; who goes to market *for* his god as it is; on whose farm nothing grows free, whose fields bear no crops, whose meadows no flowers, whose trees no fruit, but dollars; who loves not the beauty of his fruits, whose fruits are not ripe for him till they are turned to dollars. Give me the poverty that enjoys true wealth.—*Walden*

September 26, 1854

Some single red maples are very splendid now, the whole tree
bright-scarlet against the cold green pines; now when very few trees are
changed, a most remarkable object in the landscape; seen a mile off.
It is too fair to be believed, especially seen against the light. Some are
a reddish or else greenish yellow, others with red or yellow cheeks.
I suspect that the yellow maples had not scarlet blossoms.

October 24, 1858

The brilliant autumnal colors are red and yellow and the various tints, hues, and shades of these. Blue is reserved to be the color of the sky, but yellow and red are the colors of the earth-flower. Every fruit, on ripening, and just before its fall, acquires a bright tint. So do the leaves; so the sky before the end of the day, and the year near its setting. October is the red sunset sky, November the later twilight. Color stands for all ripeness and success. We have dreamed that the hero should carry his color aloft, as a symbol of the ripeness of his virtue. The noblest feature, the eye, is the fairest-colored, the jewel of the body.

October 9, 1857

It has come to this, — that the lover of art is one, and the lover of nature another, though true art is but the expression of our love of nature. It is monstrous when one cares but little about trees and much about Corinthian columns, and yet this is exceedingly common.

November 13, 1858

It is wonderful what gradation and harmony there is in nature. The light reflected from bare twigs at this season—i.e., since they began to be bare, in the latter part of October—is not only like that from gossamer, but like that which will ere long be reflected from the ice that will incrust them. So the bleached herbage of the fields is like frost, and frost like snow, and one prepares for the other.

On fields o'er which the reaper's hand has passed,
Lit by the harvest moon and autumn sun,
My thoughts like stubble floating in the wind
And of such fineness as October airs,
There, after harvest, could I glean my life,
A richer harvest reaping without toil,
And weaving gorgeous fancies at my will,
In subtler webs than finest summer haze.

—*Journal,* undated

Time is but the stream I go a-fishing in. I drink at it; but while I drink
I see the sandy bottom and detect how shallow it is. Its thin current slides
away, but eternity remains. I would drink deeper; fish in the sky,
whose bottom is pebbly with stars. I cannot count one. I know not the
first letter of the alphabet. I have always been regretting
that I was not as wise as the day I was born. — *Walden*

September 27, 1857

. . . blackberry vines here and there in sunny places look like a streak of blood on the grass.

October 24, 1837

Every part of nature teaches that the passing away of one life
is the making room for another. The oak dies down to the ground,
leaving within its rind a rich virgin mould, which will impart a vigorous
life to an infant forest. The pine leaves a sandy and sterile soil,
the harder woods a strong and fruitful mould.
So this constant abrasion and decay makes the soil of our future growth.
As I live now so shall I reap. If I grow pines and birches,
my virgin mould will not sustain the oak; but pines and birches, or,
perchance, weeds and brambles, will constitute my second growth.

October 2, 1857

Sitting on a rock east of Trillium Woods, I perceive that,
generally speaking, it is only the lower edge or *pediment* of the woods
that shows the bright autumnal tints yet, the birches, very young oaks and
hickories, huckleberry bushes, blackberries, etc., that stand around
the edges, though here and there some taller maple flames upward amid
the masses of green, or some other riper and mellower tree.

October 3, 1858

Standing on the railroad I look across the pond to Pine Hill,
where the outside trees and the shrubs scattered generally through the
wood glow through the green, yellow, and scarlet, like fires
just kindled at the base of the trees,—a general conflagration just fairly
under way, soon to envelop every tree. The hillside forest is all aglow
along its edge and in all its cracks and fissures, and soon the
flames will leap upwards to the tops of the tallest trees.

October 4, 1859

How interesting now, by wall-sides and on open springy hillsides, the large, straggling tufts of the dicksonia fern above the leaf-strewn greensward, the cold, fall-green sward! They are unusually preserved about the Corner Spring, considering the earliness of this year. Long, handsome lanceolate green fronds, pointing in every direction, recurved and full of fruit, intermixed with yellowish and sere brown and shriveled ones. The whole clump, perchance, strewn with fallen and withered maple leaves and overtopped by now withered and unnoticed osmundas. Their lingering greenness is so much the more noticeable now that the leaves (generally) have changed. They affect us as if they were evergreen, such persistent life and greenness in the midst of their own decay. . . . No matter how much withered they are, with withered leaves that have fallen on them, moist and green they spire above them, not fearing the frosts, fragile as they are. Their greenness so much the more interesting because so many have already fallen and we know that the first severer frost will cut off them too. In the summer greenness is cheap; now it is something comparatively rare and is the emblem of life to us.

October 7, 1857

I saw, by a peculiar intention or dividing of the eye, a very striking subaqueous rainbow-like phenomenon. . . . Those brilliant shrubs, which were from three to a dozen feet in height, were all reflected, dimly so far as the details of leaves, etc., were concerned, but brightly as to color, and, of course, in the order in which they stood,— scarlet, yellow, green, etc.; but, there being a slight ripple on the surface, these reflections were not true to their height though true to their breadth, but were extended downward with mathematical perpendicularity, three or four times too far, forming sharp pyramids of the several colors, gradually reduced to mere dusky points. The effect of this prolongation of the reflection was a very pleasing softening and blending of the colors, especially when a small bush of one bright tint stood directly before another of a contrary and equally bright tint. It was just as if you were to brush firmly aside with your hand or a brush a fresh line of paint of various colors, or so many lumps of friable colored powders.

October 16, 1857

A great part of the pine-needles have just fallen. See the carpet of pale-brown needles under this pine. How light it lies upon the grass, and that great rock, and the wall, resting thick on its top and its shelves, and on the bushes and underwood, hanging lightly! They are not yet flat and reddish, but a more delicate pale brown, and lie up light as joggle-sticks, just dropped. The ground is nearly concealed by them. How beautifully they die, making cheerfully their annual contribution to the soil! They fall to rise again; as if they knew that it was not one annual deposit alone that made this rich mold in which pine trees grow. They live in the soil whose fertility and bulk they increase, and in the forests that spring from it.

I mark the summer's swift decline;
The springing sward its grave-clothes weaves.
Oh, could I catch the sounds remote!
Could I but tell to human ear
The strains which on the breezes float
And sing the requiem of the dying year!

—*Journal,* undated

October 10, 1858

The simplest and most lumpish fungus has a peculiar interest to us, compared with a mere mass of earth, because it is so obviously organic and related to ourselves, however remote. It is the expression of an idea; growth according to a law; matter not dormant, not raw, but inspired, appropriated by spirit. If I take up a handful of earth, however separately interesting the particles may be, their relation to one another appears to be that of mere juxtaposition generally. I might have thrown them together thus. But the humblest fungus betrays a life akin to our own. It is a successful poem in its kind. There is suggested something superior to any particle of matter, in the idea or mind which uses and arranges the particles.

October 17, 1858

Methinks the reflections are never purer and more distinct than now at the season of the fall of the leaf, just before the cool twilight has come, when the air has a finer grain. Just as our mental reflections are more distinct at this season of the year, when the evenings grow cool and lengthen and our winter evenings with their brighter fires may be said to begin.

October 31, 1857

They stay as if to keep up the spirits of the cold-blooded frogs which
have not yet gone into the mud; that the summer may die with decent and
graceful moderation, gradually. Is not the water of the spring
improved by their presence? They fall back and droop here and there,
like the plumes of departing summer,—of the departing year.
Even in them I feel an argument for immortality. Death is so far from
being universal. The same destroyer does not destroy all. How valuable
they are (with the lycopodiums) for cheerfulness. Greenness at the end of
the year, after the fall of the leaf, as in a hale old age.
To my eyes they are tall and noble as palm groves, and always some
forest nobleness seems to have its haunt under their unbrage. . . .
All that was immortal in the swamp's herbage seems here crowded into
smaller compass,—the concentrated greenness of the swamp.
How dear they must be to the chickadee and the rabbit! The cool,
slowly retreating rear-guard of the swamp army. What virtue is theirs
that enables them to resist the frost?

November 1, 1855

This is the aspect under which the Musketaquid might be represented at this season: a long, smooth lake, reflecting the bare willows and button beeches, the stubble, and the wool-grass on its tussock, a muskrat-cabin or two conspicuously on its margin amid the unsightly tops of pontederia, and a bittern disappearing on undulating wing around a bend.

November 8, 1858

It is remarkable how little any but a lichenist will observe on the bark of trees. The mass of men have but the vaguest and most indefinite notion of mosses, as a sort of shreds and fringes, and the world in which the lichenist dwells is much further from theirs than one side of this earth from the other. They see bark as if they saw it not. . . .

Each phase of nature, while not invisible, is yet not too distinct and obtrusive. It is there to be found when we look for it, but not demanding our attention. It is like a silent but sympathizing companion in whose company we retain most of the advantages of solitude, with whom we can walk and talk, or be silent, naturally, without the necessity of talking in a strain foreign to the place.

I know of but one or two persons with whom I can afford to walk. With most the walk degenerates into a more vigorous use of your legs, ludicrously purposeless, while you are discussing some mighty argument, each one having his say, spoiling each other's day, worrying one another with conversation. . . . I know of no use in the walking part in this case, except that we may seem to be getting on together towards some goal; but of course we keep our original distance all the way. Jumping every wall and ditch with vigor in the vain hope of shaking your companion off. Trying to kill two birds with one stone, though they sit at opposite points of compass, to see nature and do the honors to one who does not.

October 25, 1852

. . . Some small bushy white asters still survive.
The autumnal tints grow gradually darker and duller, but not less rich
to my eye. And now a hillside near the river exhibits the darkest,
crispy reds and browns of every hue, all agreeably blended.
At the foot, next the meadow, stands a front rank of smoke-like maples
bare of leaves, intermixed with yellow birches. Higher up, are red oaks
of various shades of dull red, with yellowish, perhaps black oaks
intermixed, and walnuts, now brown, and near the hilltop,
or rising above the rest, perhaps, a still yellow oak, and here and there
amid the rest or in the foreground on the meadow, dull ashy
salmon-colored white oaks large and small, all these contrasting
with the clear liquid, sempiternal green of pines.

July 25, 1851

It is the most perfect seashore I have seen. The rockweed falls over you like the tresses of mermaids, and you see the propriety of that epithet. You cannot swim among these weeds and pull yourself up by them without thinking of mermen and mermaids.

November 25, 1850

The landscape looked singularly clean and pure and dry, the air,
like a pure glass, being laid over the picture, the trees so tidy, and stripped
of their leaves; the meadows and pastures, clothed with clean
dry grass, looked as if they had been swept; ice on the water and winter
in the air, but yet not a particle of snow on the ground. The woods,
divested in great part of their leaves, are being ventilated.
It is the season of perfect works, of hard, tough, ripe twigs, not of tender
buds and leaves. The leaves have made their wood, and a myriad
new withes stand up all around pointing to the sky, able to survive the
cold. It is only the perennial that you see, the iron age of the year.

WINTER

December 30, 1851

This afternoon, being on Fair Haven Hill, I heard the sound of a saw, and soon after from the Cliff saw two men sawing down a noble pine beneath, about forty rods off. . . the last of a dozen or more which were left when the forest was cut and for fifteen years have waved in solitary majesty over the sprout-land. I saw them like beavers or insects gnawing at the trunk of this noble tree, the diminutive manikins with their cross-cut saw which could scarcely span it. . . . I watch closely to see when it begins to move. Now the sawers stop, and with an axe open it a little on the side towards which it leans, that it may break the faster, and now their saw goes again. Now surely it is going; it is inclined one quarter of the quadrant, and, breathless, I expect its crashing fall. But no, I was mistaken; it has not moved an inch; it stands at the same angle as at first. It is fifteen minutes yet to its fall. Still its branches wave in the wind, as if it were destined to stand for a century, and the wind soughs through its needles as of yore; it is still a forest tree, the most majestic tree that waves over Musketaquid. The silvery sheen of sunlight is reflected from its needles; it still affords an inaccessable crotch for the squirrel's nest; not a lichen has forsaken its mast-like stem, its raking mast,—the hill is the hulk. Now, now's the moment! The manikins at its base are fleeing from their crime. They have dropped the guilty saw and axe. How slowly and majestically it starts! As if it were only swayed by a summer breeze, and would return without a sigh to its location in the air. And now it fans the hillside with its fall, and lies down to its bed in the valley, from which it is never to rise, as softly as a feather, folding its green mantle about it like a warrior, as if, tired of standing, it embraces the earth with silent joy, returning its elements to the dust again. But, hark! . . . You only saw, but did not hear. There now comes up a deafening crash to these rocks, advertising you that even trees do not die without a groan. . . . It is lumber. . . . When the fish hawk in the spring revisits the banks of the Muskatequid, he will circle in vain to find his accustomed perch, and the hen-hawk will mourn for the pines lofty enough to protect his brood. . . . I hear no knell tolled, I see no procession of mourners in the streets, or the woodland aisles. The squirrel has leaped to another tree; the hawk has circled farther off, and has now settled upon a new eyrie, but the woodman is preparing [to] lay his axe to the root of that also.

January 2, 1859

Going up the hill through Stow's young oak woodland, I listen
to the sharp, dry rustle of the withered oak leaves. This is the voice of
the wood now. It would be comparatively still and more dreary here in
other respects, if it were not for these leaves that hold on.
It sounds like the roar of the sea, and is enlivening and inspiriting like
that, suggesting how all the land is sea-coast to the aerial ocean.
It is the sound of the surf, the rut of an unseen ocean, billows of air
breaking on the forest like water on itself or on sand and rocks.
It rises and falls, wells and dies away, with agreeable alteration as the sea
surf does. Perhaps the landsman can foretell a storm by it. It is remarkable
how universal these grand murmurs are, these backgrounds of sound,—
the surf, the wind in the forest, waterfalls, etc.,—which yet to
the ear and in their origin are essentially one voice, the earth-voice, the
breathing or snoring of the creature. The earth is our ship, and this is the
sound of the wind in her rigging as we sail. Just as the inhabitant of
Cape Cod hears the surf ever breaking on its shores, so we countrymen
hear this kindred surf on the leaves of the forest.

January 24, 1856

I have seen many a collection of stately elms which better deserved to be
represented at the General Court than the manikins beneath,—
than the barroom and victualling cellar and groceries they overshadowed.
When I see their magnificent domes, miles away in the horizon, over
intervening valleys and forests, they suggest a village, a community, there.
But, after all, it is a secondary consideration whether there are
human dwellings beneath them; these may have long since passed away.
I find that into my idea of the village has entered more of the elm than of
the human being. They are worth many a political borough.
They constitute a borough. The poor human representative of his party
sent out from beneath their shade will not suggest a tithe of the
dignity, the true nobleness and comprehensiveness of view, the
sturdiness and independence, and serene beneficence that they do.
They look from township to township. . . . They battle with the
tempests of a century. See what scars they bare, what limbs they lost
before we were born! Yet they never adjourn; they steadily vote for their
principles, and send their roots farther and wider from the same center.
They die at their posts, and they leave a tough butt for the choppers
to exercise themselves about, and a stump which serves for their
monument. They attend no caucus, they make no compromise, they use
no policy. Their one principle is growth. They combine a true
radicalism with a true conservatism. Their radicalism is not a cutting
away of roots, but an infinite multiplication and extension of them under
all surrounding institutions. They take a firmer hold on the earth that they
may rise higher into the heavens. . . . Their conservatism is a dead
but solid heart-wood, which is the pivot and firm column of support to all
this growth, appropriating nothing to itself, but forever by its support
assisting to extend the area of their radicalism. Half a century
after they are dead at the core, they are preserved by radical reforms.
They do not, like men, from radicals turn conservatives. Their
conservative part dies out first; their radical and growing part survives.
They acquire new States and Territories, while the old dominions decay,
and become the habitation of bears and owls and coons.

January 4, 1853

In the twilight I went through the swamp, and the yellow birches
sent forth a dull-yellow gleam which each time made my heart beat faster.
Occasionally you come to a dead and leaning white birch, beset
with large fungi like ears or little shelves, with a rounded edge above.
I walked with the yellow birch. The prinos is green within. If there were
Druids whose temples were the oak groves, my temple is the swamp.
Sometimes I was in doubt about a birch whose vest was
buttoned smooth and dark, till I came nearer and saw the yellow
gleaming through, or where a button was off.

March 9, 1852

Again it rains, and I turn about.
The sounds of water falling on rocks and of air falling on trees
are very much alike.
Though cloudy, the air excites me. Yesterday all was tight as a stricture
on my breast; to-day all is loosened. It is a different element
from what it was. The sides of the bushy hill where the snow is melted
look, through this air, as if I were under the influence of some
intoxicating liquor. The earth is not quite steady nor palpable
to my senses, a little idealized.

January 21, 1853

I wish to hear the silence of the night, for the silence is something positive and to be heard. I cannot walk with my ears covered. I must stand still and listen with open ears, far from the noises of the village, that the night may make its impression on me. A fertile and eloquent silence. Sometimes the silence is merely negative, an arid and barren waste in which I shudder, where no ambrosia grows. I must hear the whispering of a myriad voices. Silence alone is worthy to be heard. Silence is of various depths and fertility, like soil. Now it is a mere Sahara, where men perish of hunger and thirst, now a fertile bottom, or prairie, of the West. As I leave the village, drawing nearer to the woods, I listen from time to time to hear the hounds of Silence baying the Moon, — to know if they are on the track of any game. If there's no Diana in the night, what is it worth? . . . The silence rings; it is musical and thrills me. A night in which the silence was audible. I heard the unspeakable.

January 12, 1855

Perhaps what most moves us in winter is some reminiscence of
far-off summer. . . . What beauty in the running brooks! What life!
What society! The cold is merely superficial; it is summer still at the
core, far, far within. It is in the cawing of the crow, the crowing of the
cock, the warmth of the sun on our backs. I hear faintly the cawing
of a crow far, far away, echoing from some unseen wood-side,
as if deadened by the springlike vapor which the sun is drawing from
the ground. It mingles with the slight murmur of the village, the sound of
children at play, as one stream empties gently into another,
and the wild and tame are one. What a delicious sound! It is not merely
crow calling to crow, for it speaks to me too. I am part of one
great creature with him; if he has voice, I have ears. I can hear
when he calls, and have engaged not to shoot nor stone him
if he will caw to me each spring.

January 5, 1856

The thin snow now driving from the north and lodging on my coat
consists of those beautiful star crystals, . . . Nature is full of genius, full
of the divinity; so that not a snowflake escapes its fashioning hand.
. . . The same law that shapes the earth-star shapes the snow-star.
As surely as the petals of a flower are fixed, each of these countless
snow-stars comes whirling to earth, pronouncing thus, with emphasis, the
number six. Order, κοσμος. . . .

What a world we live in! where myriads of these little disks, so
beautiful to the most prying eye, are whirled down on every traveler's
coat, the observant and the unobservant, and on the restless squirrel's fur,
and on the far-stretching fields and forests, the wooded dells,
and the mountain-tops. Far, far away from the haunts of man, they roll
down some little slope, fall over and come to their bearings, and
melt or lose their beauty in the mass, ready anon to swell some little rill
with their contribution, and so, at last, the universal ocean from which
they came. There they lie, like the wreck of chariot-wheels after
a battle in the skies. Meanwhile the meadow mouse shoves them aside
in his gallery, the schoolboy casts them in his snowball, or the
woodman's sled glides smoothly over them, these glorious spangles,
the sweepings of heaven's floor. And they all sing, melting as they sing
of the mysteries of the number six,—six, six, six. He takes up
the waters of the sea in his hand, leaving the salt; He disperses it in
mist through the skies; He recollects and sprinkles it like grain in
six-rayed snowy stars over the earth, there to lie till
He dissolves its bonds again.

January 7, 1857

But alone in distant woods or fields, in unpretending sproutlands
or pastures tracked by rabbits, even in a bleak and, to most, cheerless day,
like this, when a villager would be thinking of his inn, I come to
myself, I once more feel myself grandly related, and that cold and
solitude are friends of mine. I suppose that this value, in my case,
is equivalent to what others get by church-going and prayer. I come to my
solitary woodland walk as the homesick go home. I thus dispose of
the superfluous and see things as they are, grand and beautiful.
I have told many that I walk every day about half the daylight, but I think
they do not believe it. I wish to get the Concord, the Massachusetts,
the America, out of my head and be sane a part of every day. . . .
I wish to forget, a considerable part of every day, all mean, narrow, trivial
men. . . . , and therfore I come out to these solitudes, where the
problem of existence is simplified. I get away a mile or two from the
town into the stillness and solitude of nature, with rocks, trees,
weeds, snow about me. I enter some glade in the woods, perchance, where
a few weeds and dry leaves alone lift themselves above the surface
of the snow, and it is as if I had come to an open window.
I see out and around myself. . . . This stillness, solitude, wildness of
nature is a kind of thoroughwort, or boneset, to my intellect.
This is what I go out to seek. It is as if I always met in those places
some grand, serene, immortal, infinitely encouraging, though
invisible, companion, and walked with him.

January 7, 1852

Every day a new picture is painted and framed, held up for half an hour,
in such lights as the Great Artist chooses, and then withdrawn,
and the curtain falls.
And then the sun goes down, and long the afterglow gives light.
And then the damask curtains glow along the western window.
And now the first star is lit, and I go home.

January 26, 1853

There are from time to time mornings, both in summer and in winter, when especially the world seems to begin anew, beyond which memory need not go, for not behind them is yesterday and our past life; when, as in the morning of a hoar frost, there are visible the effects as of a certain creative energy.

. . . The world has visibly been recreated in the night. Mornings of creation, I call them. In the midst of these marks of a creative energy recently active, while the sun is rising with more than usual splendor, I look back . . . for the era of this creation, not into the night, but to a dawn for which no man ever rose early enough. A morning which carries us back beyond the Mosaic creation, where crystallizations are fresh and unmelted. It is the poet's hour. Mornings when men are new-born, men who have the seeds of life in them.

Printed in the United States of America by Barnes Press, New York City,
100# Kimberly Clark Lithofect Gloss.
Bound in Columbia Sampson linen by Sendor Bindery, New York City.
The book is set in Centaur and Arrighi (designed by Bruce Rogers)
by Mackenzie & Harris, Inc., San Francisco.
The design is by David Brower.

First published in the United States in 1988 by
The Overlook Press
Lewis Hollow Road
Woodstock, New York 12498

Library of Congress Cataloging in Publication Data

Varga, Domokos.
Budapest.

Reprint. Originally published:
Budapest: Corvina Kiadó © 1985
Translated from the Hungarian.
1. Budapest (Hungary)—Descriptions—Views.
i title
db985. v3713 1987 943.9'1 87–5808

ISBN 0–87951–288–1

Design by Zoltán Kemény
Translation by Elisabeth Hoch and J.E. Söllösy

Budapest

Domokos Varga

THE
OVERLOOK
PRESS
WOODSTOCK NEW YORK

-3-

2

3

1. *View of Budapest*
2–4. *Two river banks, but one city*

4

Buda and Pest

Many cities grace the banks of the Rhine, and as many lie along the Volga. But the Danube is the only river in Europe whose waters run through eight countries and wash the stones of three capitals. Of the three Danubian capitals, Budapest enjoys a central location. From Vienna, the river flows on and through it before continuing its course towards Belgrade. Both Vienna and Belgrade are predominantly right-bank cities. It is on the right bank of the Danube that their present-day centres have developed in the course of the centuries.

But what about Budapest?

The river that flows through this city divides it into two parts: Buda and Pest. If we trace the pulse of the city with due attention, we shall observe that its left bank appears to throb more intensely to make the centre of Pest the heart of the capital.

In Vienna, too, the Danube cuts the city in two, but only because the growing city has expanded beyond the river.
In Budapest, on the other hand, two separate cities have developed on the two banks, competing with each other and yet joined by countless ties.
Here, the Danube is much wider than in Vienna. Formerly, all river transport had to be suspended in winter, an interruption which lasted for weeks, sometimes months, Yet through the centuries, Pest was nevertheless kept alive mainly by the fact that Buda was there on the opposite bank, while Buda owed its animation to the existence of Pest across the river. More precisely, both cities owed their prosperity to the fact that since ancient times, they have represented the most convenient place for crossing the middle reaches of the Danube.
The Hungarian Plain, the famous *puszta,* stretches right up to the boundaries of Pest, which is built on the western edge of this spacious prairie. But Buda, on the right bank, is situated on the eastern border of forest-clad

6

5–6. *On the top of the hill lies the Castle District, at its foot, Watertown*
7. *Towers of the Baroque St. Anne's Church*

hills. Here, merchants arriving from various directions always found buyers for their money, gold or silver.
Lying on the plain, Pest was enabled to grow into a large city first of all by the exertions of its own craftsmen and merchants. Buda could boast a special feature: the Castle Hill rising above the Danube. From the thirteenth century on, all the kings of Hungary in the late Middle Ages resided upon the long plateau of this hilly land, and thus Buda became the centre of the government of the country.
The first permanent bridge over the Danube, the Chain Bridge, was constructed between the twin cities in the 1840s. It was only around this time that the thought of uniting Buda and Pest to form the capital of Hungary, then embarked on the road of modern development, was first seriously suggested. But the name to be given to the united city was a matter that required lengthy consideration. Some preferred to call it Pest-Buda, even before the two places had been officially united. Others referred to it as Buda-Pest. Eventually, the new city was called Budapest.

7

The official unification of Pest and Buda took place in 1872. The small territory of Óbuda (Old Buda), situated north of Buda, was also attached to the city. Together the three geographical units formed Budapest, the capital of Hungary. The new capital enjoyed equal rights with Vienna, for in 1867 Hungary acquired the rank of co-dominion with Austria within the Habsburg Empire.
Today, Budapest has six major bridges instead of one, plus one railway bridge to the north and another to the south of the city. A subway (the Metro) passes under the Danube. However, anyone heading for the opposite bank is still said to be going to "Buda" or "Pest" respectively. In the same way, it is natural for people to say "I live in Buda," or "I work in Pest". As long as Budapest exists, Buda and Pest will survive ineradicably under their old, respective names.

Perspectives

No city in the world looks equally beautiful from every angle. Thus, the particular vantage point from which one views Budapest is not irrelevant. The briefest initial exploration will reveal quite a number of unsightly houses and districts. However, thanks to the city's many well-favoured aspects, its lovely parts are even more easily discovered.
It is sufficient to halt anywhere along the Pest bank of the Danube and look across at the rows of houses, squares, churches and hills on the opposite side. Bare rocks, gardens, parks, houses of different sizes, towers, bastions and castle walls present a variegated view. But it is perhaps even better not to pause at any one point, for the scene varies constantly as we walk along the bank, giving particular appeal to the magnificent view unfolding before us. Perhaps the best is to board a river-cruise boat and enjoy the sight of both Buda and Pest simultaneously along the full length of their banks.
Viewed from the Buda side of the river, the perspective is also fascinating, especially from the top of Gellért Hill and Castle Hill. These elevations rise so abruptly over the river that river craft seem to float at their feet, and the close-packed buildings of Pest appear to be only an arm's length away.
When one has had one's fill of the view of Pest, the Danube, the islands, bridges and boats from the nearby hilltops, one can easily find a new perspective. By turning one's back on the view, after a few minutes' walk the semicircle of the more distant hills of Buda opens in the opposite direction, where thou-

9

8. *The Danube—in perspective*
9. *A view from Gellért Hill. . .*
10. *. . .from Castle Hill. . .*
11. *. . .from the Danube bank in Pest*

sands of family houses have been built into the tree-clad hillsides. Here and there some larger apartment blocks appear among them, but fortunately, these are not numerous enough as yet to spoil the unified effect of the vast landscape. Its main outlines are drawn not by human hand but by nature herself. The houses do not markedly disrupt the ridges of the hills, nor is the effect of the high places reduced by skyscrapers. Both these circumstances enhance the charm of the view.

The highest peak to be seen is János-hegy. This 528 metres high forested area is situated within the boundaries of Budapest. It is topped by a look-out tower with a terrace which commands a circular view which is unique in the capital. Eastwards, Budapest stretches out far below, while to the north, south and west the mountainous region of Buda undulates in the hazy distance.

10

11

12

Neither Buda, nor Pest

The Danube, its islands, boats and bridges belong neither to Buda nor to Pest.
The title of the famous "Blue Danube" waltz is deceptive. The river is not blue, not even in Vienna, and still less in Budapest. However, the camera does not believe the human eye, and always depicts the greenish-grey river in more vivid hues.
The Danube does not owe its colour to the pollution that is the byproduct of modernization. It is natural to it, and is probably produced by the quantity of fine grains of sand floating in the water. Every river carries large quantities of alluvial material: stones, pebbles, sand and silt, but where its current slackens, it always deposits part of these. The river at Budapest was suitable for such deposits in two particularly large areas. North of the city, the Danube spreads beyond its narrow bed to form the Danube Bend at Visegrád, below which it tries to rid itself of part of its burden by creating Szentendre Island, which stretches for over 30 km as far as Budapest. This is followed by a number of smaller islands within the area of the capital. The next 5 or 6 km of the river has no islands, since the Danube cuts the city centre in two.

13

12–13. *On and above the river*
14. *Towards Margaret Island*
15. *Here the boats must fight the tide*
16. *Waiting for a boat*

Then at its lower reaches, it forms the 50 km long Csepel Island.

The ferry between Buda and Pest once attracted itinerant merchants, cattle drovers and travellers because here they could cross directly from one bank to the other, whereas if they travelled through the islanded reaches, they would have had to cross two branches of the river.

True, ferry-men here had to cope with a much stronger current. Castle Hill and Gellért Hill, both rising on the Buda bank, narrow the river bed. They apply spurs to its flank, like a rider urging his steed to a gallop.

This explains why there are no islands in this section of the river. The first bridge was also built at this point, because it could accommodate the shortest span. After Szentendre, Margaret Island is the most beautiful and the best known among the smaller Danube islands. Its southern tip extends right into the heart of the city. Earlier it was eroded by the strong current of the Danube. Above its northern tip, closer to Pest, there once stood an islet called Fürdő Sziget (Bathing Island) with several thermal springs; however, it was gradually washed away by the river. But Margaret Island was large enough to survive. What the river washed away from its upper

17

17. *Margaret Island*
18. *Entrance to the Island*

end, it always deposited lower down. Thus, the island kept "swimming" downward about 2 cm a year, until it was fixed in place with bridges; then both its flanks were faced with stone slabs to set it at rest.

Today, the island is a quiet and restful retreat in the busy city. It forms, in effect, one huge park with many old trees and miriads of flowers. Its bushes are lovers' hideaways, its lawns playgrounds; old people rest on its benches. Private cars are banned, except for vehicles bound for the hotels situated at the northern end of the island, which can be approached over Árpád Bridge.

When the inhabitants of Budapest say to each

18

19

19–23. *There's not another haven like it in the bustling capital*

21

20

22

other "Let's go to the Island," or "Let's meet tomorrow on the Island," they always mean Margaret Island. For them, it is *the* island, the one and only island of the capital.

There are bathing facilities, tennis courts, an open-air theatre and cinema, an old and a new thermal hotel, restaurants, a small zoo, all of which fortunately do not occupy too much space on the more than 2 km long island. Plenty of room remains for the park. The park is the most important feature of the island. Strict building regulations ensure its preservation as the most tranquil and most highly frequented green area within Budapest.

24

25

26

24. *The thermal lake*
25. *The former church of the Premonstratensians*
26–29. *Joys on the island and by the riverside*

27

28

29

The park is much more than a public garden; it carries many historic associations. In the Middle Ages it was the site of a Dominican convent in which the daughter of King Béla IV (1235–1270) took the veil. After the great Mongolian devastation in 1241–1242, this thirteenth-century Hungarian king, who is also called "the builder of the nation," built a castle for himself in Buda. The Princess, whose name was Margaret, lived out her brief, ascetic life in such piety, and performed so many good deeds attended by divine miracles, that she was beatified and later canonized by the Church. The island is named in honour of her memory. Earlier, it was called the Isle of Hares. The ruins of the ancient Dominican convent and church are still extant.

Near the Dominican convent stood the church of the Premonstratensian friars. Part of its twelfth-century foundations and walls have survived. The church was reconstructed in the Romanesque style in the 1930s. In the centre of the island, next to the Rose Garden, stand the ruins of a fourteenth-century Franciscan church.

Bridges. Boats. Harbours. A floating restaurant on a decommissioned boat. Here and there, riverside anglers grown stiff from im-

30

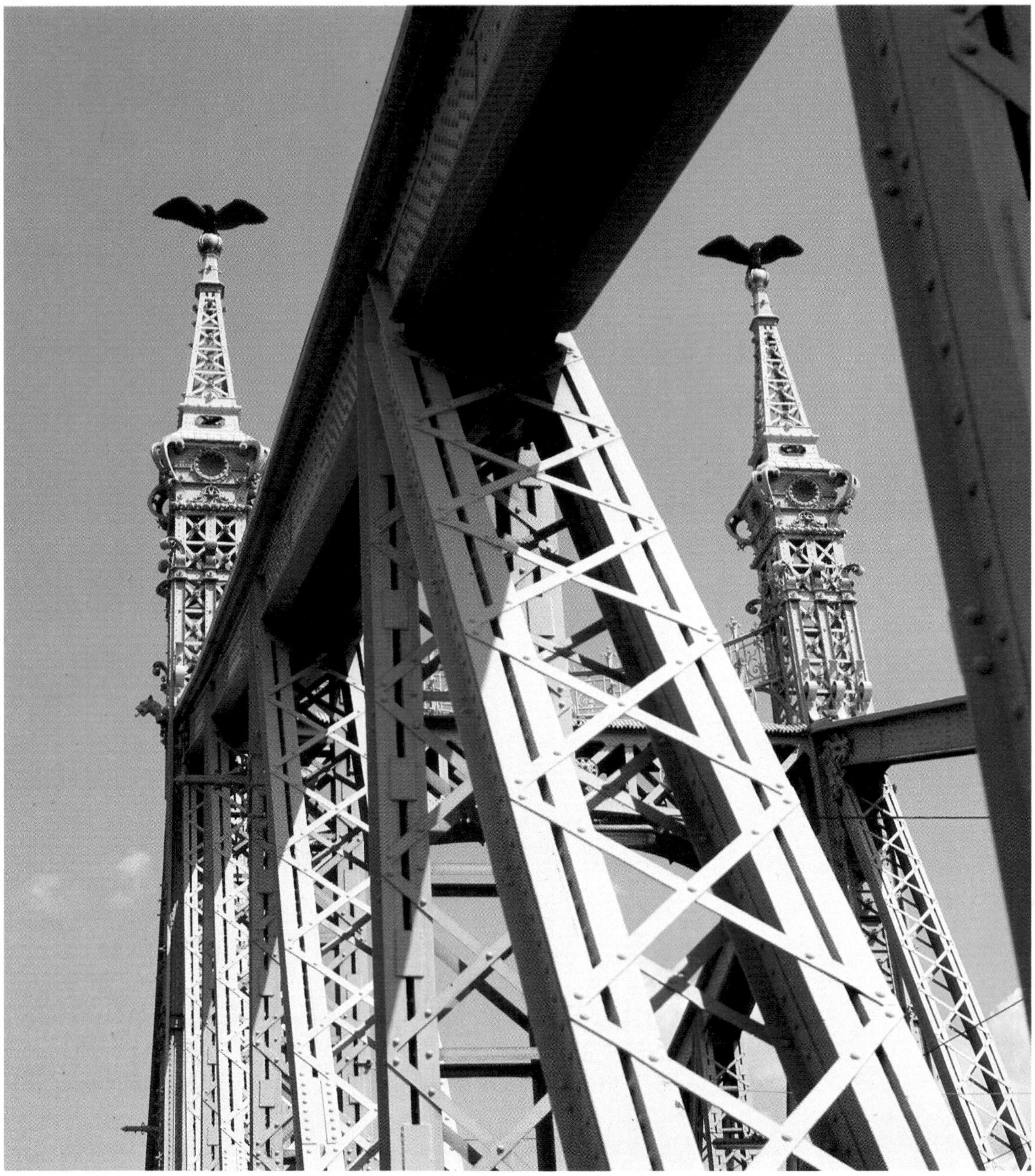

mobility scrutinize the surface of the river with endless patience for a catch. Obliviously, young couples kiss; schoolboys study; children play with pebbles on the steps leading down to the water's edge.

But here again, it is the city with its variety of buildings that attracts our attention. The two banks, Pest and Buda. Or Buda and Pest.

Formerly Ferenc József Bridge

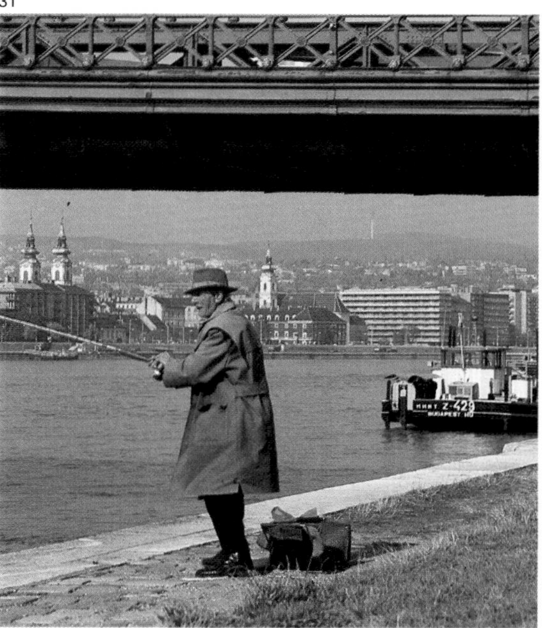

30. *Liberty Bridge with the* turul *birds*
31. *By the river, you can always find a fisherman or two with infinite patience*
32. *As if it had been rising above the river since time immemorial...*

31

The bridges spanning the river

Looked at with the eyes of a local inhabitant, the bridges are part of the familiar view of Budapest. It is as if they had joined the two banks of the river since times immemorial, and that nothing could destroy either their slender bodies or their massive stone pillars. Yet there are witnesses aplenty who had seen the bridges destroyed by expertly placed demolition charges in the winter of 1944–1945. They were destroyed because Hitler had

32

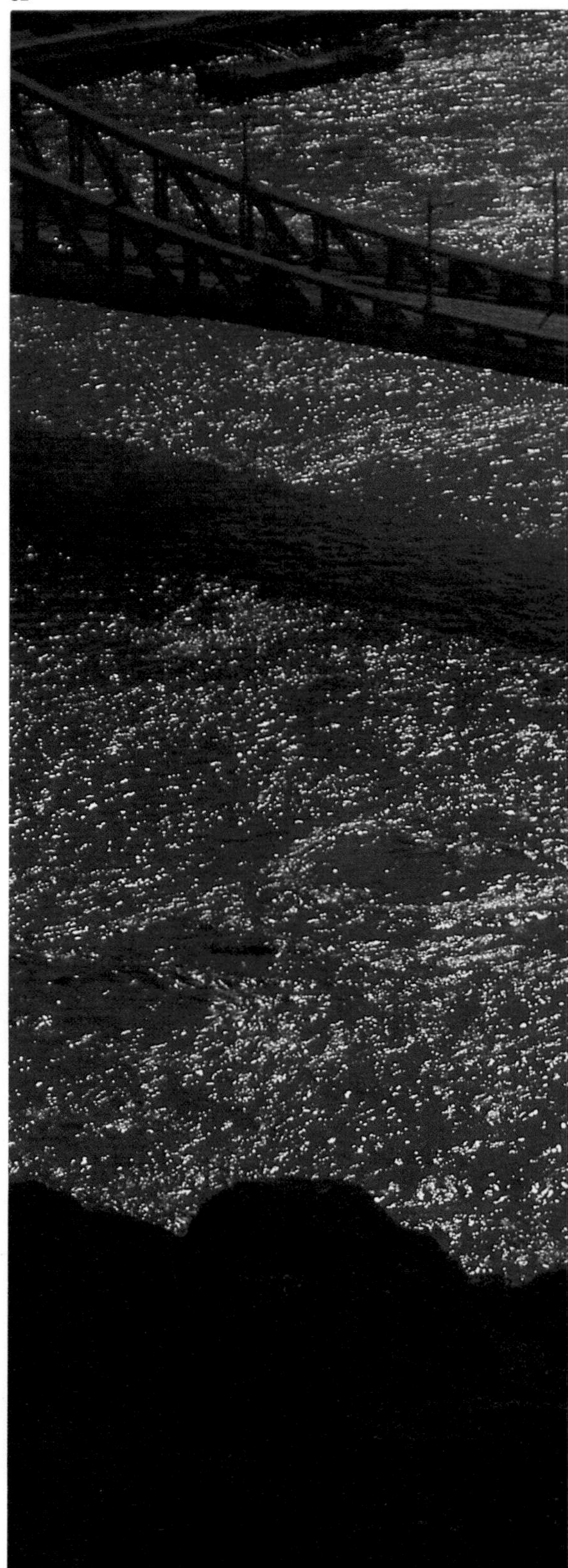

ordered the German troops then surrounded in Budapest to hold out to the last against the besieging Soviet army. That the Germans were driven from Pest to more easily defensible Buda ensured the ruin of the Danube bridges.

True, it ensured their own ruin as well. The ruin of those who blew up the bridges, who died in obedience to orders, and who were responsible for the deaths of so many thousands of hungry old women and children.

The dead are buried, but the bridges stand again, showing none of the signs of the earlier destruction.

Yes, they seem to have spanned the river since time immemorial. From north to south, they are: the Árpád Bridge, Margaret Bridge, the Chain Bridge, Elizabeth Bridge, Liberty (Szabadság) Bridge and Petőfi Bridge. Budapest is unimaginable without them.

The bridges are indispensable; in fact, we could do with more. For the people of Budapest, they not only provide faster transport and communication between the city and the

34

35

country; they belong to the city's scape. This applies especially to Margaret Bridge resting upon the southern part of Margaret Island, and, the Chain Bridge and Liberty Bridge.
Margaret Bridge, which is over a hundred years old, spans the river in a rather unusual V-form, for this was the only solution permitting the construction of a third abutment leading onto the island.
Except for being somewhat wider, today's Chain Bridge is an exact replica of the original bridge built in the 1840s. It appears to continue into the tunnel running under Castle Hill. According to the story told to credulous children, the bridge is pushed into the tunnel at night, and when it is raining.
Many humorous stories abound about this oldest permanent bridge of Budapest. One of them comes from the times when the Hun-

33. *The arch of Elizabeth Bridge on the Pest side of the river*
34. *The axis of Margaret Bridge is interrupted at the southern tip of Margaret Island*
35. *An allegorical being guards the water from each pillar*

36

37

38

39

garian nobility was still discussing its possible construction. Was the bridge needed or not? Those who were for building it tried to canvas for as many supporters of the project as possible. But an old nobleman whom they tried to persuade to vote in favour of it, urging him how nice it would be to cross the river safely even in the dead of winter, merely waved his hand sadly, and said with wise resignation: "What is the good of it for the little time I have left?"
The southern neighbour of the Chain Bridge, the Elizabeth Bridge, was built – in its original form, at least – at the turn of the century.

36. *From the Chain Bridge the road leads into the tunnel under Castle Hill*
37. *The stone lions of the Chain Bridge*
38–40. *Elizabeth Bridge, the city's most graceful bridge*

Agip

41

42

41–42. *István Széchenyi (1791–1860) initiated the construction of the first permanent bridge. The Chain Bridge recalls his memory*
43–44. *For the people of Budapest, the bridges are more than "works of art" . . .*

43

It came to be regarded as the finest bridge in Budapest. But the one now replacing the original is perhaps even lighter and more graceful than the pre-war structure, and appears to float above the river.

South of Elizabeth Bridge stood the bridge named after Francis Joseph, the Habsburg Emperor and one-time King of Hungary. It was reconstructed in 1946 in almost the same form as before, but its name was changed to Liberty (Szabadság) Bridge. Thus it evokes the spirit of the end of the century, while its name is associated with the post-war years.

Hills and thermal springs

One may ask why such a long stretch of the Danube flows almost directly north to south, and why it flows through Budapest in the

44

45. *Bridges over the Danube*

same direction. According to geologists, a characteristic fault-line in the earth's crust determined the course of the river. The geological layers west of this line became slightly more raised, while those east of it sank somewhat.

It appears that the course of the Danube cuts off the hills of Buda from the territory on its eastern bank. It is enough to look at the barren rocks of Gellért Hill to understand the natural forces that must have been active here in earlier times. The slope of Castle Hill overlooking the river is also steep enough to bring to mind the former movements of the earth's crust in this region.

Buda owes its hilly aspect to these early earth tremors, as does the flat land of Pest which became filled with river ballast, sand and mud. A sunken hilly region, the counterpart and direct continuation of the Buda hills, lies

47

48

46

buried beneath these layers. It is composed of the same dolomite, limestone and marl. And so, in addition to the bridges and the Metro tunnel, Buda and Pest are connected by the masses of rock which form the hills of Buda and Pest beneath the river at increasing depth as they approach the latter.

Apart from being interesting from a scientific point of view, these circumstances have their practical significance as well, namely, in the exploration for thermal springs.

Budapest owes its abudance of thermal waters to the same geological fault-line which played such an important role in the development of the Danube's bed. Presumably, a series of earthquakes broke up pre-existing huge masses of rock which then slipped apart to create fissures that made it possible for immense quantities of hot water to well up without hindrance from the deep. In Buda these emerged at the surface in the form of springs; in Pest they rose only as far as the buried dolomite layers.

Hungary is the land of thermal springs. There is hardly any part of her territory where drilling deep would fail to bring thermal water to the surface. The first explorations to this end were carried out in the 1860s. Budapest was included right from the beginning, as Buda had been famous for its natural hot springs long before. It was remembered that thermal waters had existed on the small islet which had disappeared near the northern end of Margaret Island; thus exploratory drillings were attempted on Margaret Island, too. The 44°C water that rises from a depth of 118 metres, originated from a layer of dolomite similar to that from which Buda's natural thermal springs emerged.

The next explorations were carried out in

50

49

51

46. *The Palatinus spa on Margaret Island*
47–48. *The Gellért and Rudas Baths receive their waters from the thermal springs on the Buda side of the Danube bank*
49. *The Lukács Baths and Pool*
50. *The Széchenyi Baths in City Park*
51. *In the medicinal waters of the Széchenyi Spa*

Városliget, the large City Park in Pest, about three kilometres from the Danube. With the rudimentary equipment of those times, the drilling took several years; finally it was successful and a thermal spring of 74° C gushed forth from a depth of almost a thousand metres, again, originating in the dolomite layer.

Since then Pest has several other thermal wells and also thermal baths fed by them. Many of Hungary's thermal springs have a curative effect, and Budapest may rightly be called a city of spas. Visitors have continued to come here primarily for the sake of their health, to take advantage of the various services offered by the thermal baths.

53

52

In praise of the hillsides

City buildings always divide space into vertical and horizontal planes. This applies to New York as it does to Budapest or Melbourne. Of course, roofs may be slanting, and various elements of buildings may have other than plane surfaces, but this will not change the priority of and emphasis upon the vertical and horizontal planes.

The human spirit finds it difficult to bear the depressing dominance of vertical and horizontal planes and the rectangular corners and angles so characteristic of large cities. The greatest achievements of architecture — in the pyramids, colonnades, porticos, vaulting, domes, apses, pagoda-roofs, as well as the innovations introduced with the Gothic and Baroque styles — all seem to have sought some sort of remedy — the resolution of the apparent constraint imposed by a spatial order governed by gravitation — in various other solutions for breaking up the space we inhabit. The spectacle of artificial slopes formed by stairways generally creates such an effect.

But how much more does the sight of natural slopes, the natural domes of mountain peaks, or the pagoda-roof angles formed by the valleys between them, the steeply falling rocky mountainsides with peristyles formed by multitudes of living trees and the Baroque-style ornaments presented by their knotted forms and branches!

It is invaluable for a city to be rich in such natural features, and unforgivable not to

54

make the best use of them. We must admit that Budapest is not altogether blameless in the construction of buildings that do not harmonize sufficiently with the lines of its peaks and ridges. However, the city's location is so favourable that the greater part of its natural features have survived in spite of all the errors. This goes not only for the city's overall aspect and open perspectives, but for its details as well.

Castle Hill is somewhat more densely built up than the other hillsides, but even here a sense of liberation from the confinement of the "main planes" of the city can be felt. And this is even more the case with Gellért Hill and Sashegy.

55

57

56

52–57. *In praise of the rows of steps*

59

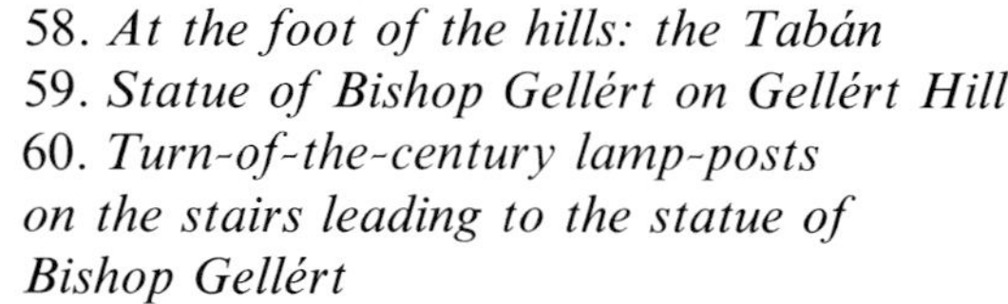

58. *At the foot of the hills: the Tabán*
59. *Statue of Bishop Gellért on Gellért Hill*
60. *Turn-of-the-century lamp-posts on the stairs leading to the statue of Bishop Gellért*
61. *The main figure of the Liberation Monument*

61

60

Gellért Hill is named after an Italian bishop, the righ-hand man of the first Christian king of Hungary, St. Stephen (1001—1038), who worked zealously for the organization of the Church and the conversion to Christianity of the Magyars. St. Stephen' s statue surmounts Castle hill, that of St. Gellért the hill named after him, near the spot whence—according to legend—insurgent pagans rolled the pious bishop down into the Danube in a barrel lined with spikes.

Today, when one makes one's way down the lower gradient of the south-western slope, the soothing sight of fig trees with abudant fruit divert the spirit. It is such a surprise that one wonders how figs got there at all!

They are probably of Italian origin and most likely left their homeland even before the saintly bishop. In fact, it is presumed that they were transplanted to this cooler country by settlers coming to Pannonia from the Roman Empire.

They have been thriving here ever since,

together with the sweet chestnut trees, also of Italian origin, growing sufficiently well hereabouts as evidence that the Mediterranean climate makes itself felt even in the surroundings of Budapest.

This is due mainly to the Carpathians, which border Hungary and hinder the inrush of cold air from the north and north-east into the central Danube valley. To these likewise Budapest owes its comparatively mild winters, as well its fairly dry sunny early autumns, which last from mid September to the second

62

63

64

62. *The cable railway takes its passangers to the plateau just under the summit of János Hill*

63. *The Pioneer Railway winds its way along the forest-clad hills of Buda, up to Hűvösvölgy*

64. *But nothing beats treading a forest path on foot*

half of October, when the grapes, figs and sweet chestnuts ripen.

Once Buda also produced famous wines. But a metropolis, Budapest today no longer needs viticulture. It is more important that the expanding city should not spread across the forest-clad slopes of the hills and areas formerly occupied by vineyards; and it is important that there should remain sufficient open country for recreation.

No complaint can be raised in respect of Gellért Hill, which has the city's most beautiful parks. The neighbouring Sashegy has not been built in, and its rocky upper part has with its rare plants and animals been declared a nature conservation area. The metropolis hums far below, but peace and quiet reign on the peaks and neighbouring hillsides.

The woodlands extending uninterrupted over many thousands of acres of undeveloped undulating country, a little further from the Danube, is an even more invaluable asset of the capital. Here the gardens of the houses and the neighbouring forest merge without effort; the city does not actually end at their

66

65

67

68

69

65–67. Statuary from the late 19th century on the buildings at Nos. 9, 2, 12, Népköztársaság útja (Avenue of the People's Republic) the only true avenue of the city
68. Detail of the façade of the Academy of Music
69. Courtyard near Népköztársaság útja
70. Detail of the Opera House

70

border. Well-kept walks, grounds allocated for physical exercise, benches, small wooden shelters against sudden showers await hikers in the oak forests and beach-groves. There is also the hundred-year-old cogwheel railway running its winding course some 12.5 km in length on Szabadság (Liberty) Hill; and the cable railway, operating under the name *Libegő,* takes you almost to the very top of János Hill within a few minutes.

Rationale of the City

The hills, valleys and rivers were not created by human agency, yet they have all found their proper place. Nor was special pattern of the city designed solely on the drawing boards of engineers. The gradual expansion of settlements has its own laws, and Budapest is no exception. The main sections of the capital's two nuclei, Pest and Buda, developed along the two banks of the Danube. The people who settled needed adequate protection such as defensible stone walls could provide.
It is worth tracing the remains of these walls.

71. *Along the Avenue each house has its own character (No. 90 Avenue of the People's Republic)*
72. *The Avenue ends at Heroes' Square*

Parts of the present existing boulevard—in Buda, Mártírok útja, in Pest, the Kiskörút (Tolbuhin körút, Múzeum körút and Tanács körút)—run roughly along their ancient lines. One might say that the old town-walls determined the line of the future inner boulevards, and the boulevards, for their part, determined the points at which the Danube bridges were built.

Afterwards, the plan of the city developed accordingly. Roads like Váci út, Majakovszkij utca, Rákóczi út and Üllői út, which spread out from Budapest towards other towns, had their origin at the respective gates

71

72

73

73. Heroes' Square with the Millennial Monument

74–75. Triumphal chariots top the Monument's pillars

76–77. The square is bounded on the left by the Museum of Fine Arts and on the right by the Art Gallery

74

75

76

in the walls. So when purposeful townplanning began in Pest, it required no special wisdom on the part of the planners to develop the already established pattern of boulevards and radiating thoroughfares. In Pest, where level ground made it possible, the course of another ring, the so-called Great Boulevard (today's Ferenc körút, József körút, Lenin körút and Szent István körút), and later on a third, were mapped out and the existing radial thoroughfares were widened.
The obvious development in the lay-out of Budapest, which took place virtually of its own accord, accounts for the irregularities in the main thoroughfares mentioned above. The boulevards do not describe a perfect arc, nor—with one exception—do the radial thoroughfares take straight courses either.

77

78

79

80

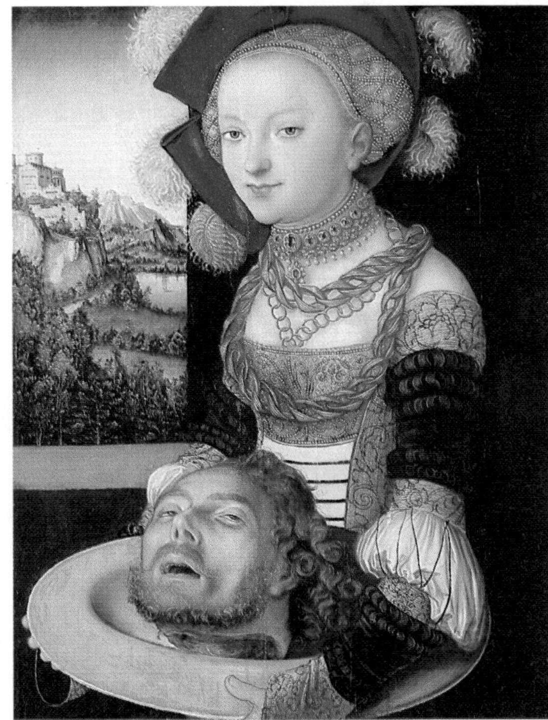

81

There is one exception which is a true avenue, the work of town-planning engineers of the last century. It was actually built the way they conceived, planned and created it. They wanted it to look the way it is.

The thoroughfare we refer to is as straight as the crow flies. It is wide. It is spacious. It is flanked by rows of trees and villas. In a single decisive leap it joins the most densely populated nucleus of the city with the beautiful open spaces of the City Park. Its original name was Sugárút (The Avenue). Now it is called Népköztársaság útja (Avenue of the People's Republic).

The thoroughfare was criticized at the time for leading to the park. Why make the city's main thoroughfare run into a park? And why close it, even before it reaches its destination, with the large expense of Heroes' Square?

But when looking at the pattern—and beauty—of the city as a whole, one has to admit that the broad thoroughfare has contributed a great deal to it. The mere fact that it broke up the crowded quarters of Pest was an important improvement; at the same time, it created a worthy setting for some fine public buildings, amongst them the Budapest Opera House built very much in the style of the Vienna Opera. Furthermore, it enabled the town-planners to develop on the fringe of City Park the most beautiful square in Pest, Hősök tere (Heroes' Square). Last but not least, it brought the Park itself closer to the heart of the city, especially after the subway—the first electric underground railway in Europe—was completed.

82

From the collection of
the Museum of Fine Arts:
78. *Leonardo da Vinci (1452–1519): Head of a Warrior (The Red Head)*
79. *Raffaello Santi (1483–1520): Portrait of Pietro Bembo*
80. *Lucas Cranach (1472–1553): Salome*
81. *Pieter Bruegel the Elder (c. 1525–1569): The Sermon of St. John the Baptist*
82. *Gustave Courbet (1819–77): Wrestlers*

83

84

85

86

83. *El Greco (1541–1614): Mary Magdalene*
84. *Francisco Jose de Goya (1746–1828): Portrait of the Wife of Juan Augustin Bermudez*
85. *Angelica Kauffmann (1741–1807): Portrait of a Lady*
86. *Camille Pissarro (1831–1903): Pont Neuf*
87. *Pablo Picasso (1881–1973): Mother and Child*

87

88

89

88–89. *Vajdahunyad Castle, the pride of City Park*
90. *The lake of City Park with the "Castle"*

90

91. *The statue of Anonymus, chronicler of King Béla III*
92. *The car of the first underground in Europe in the Underground Railway Museum, Deák Square*
93–94. *In the winter, the boating lake of City Park is turned into an ice-skating ring*
95. *The Széchenyi Bath*
96. *A green island in the heart of the city*
97–99. *The Zoo*

91

92

93

94

However, let us stop for a minute at Heroes' Square, if but for the sake of the millenial monument whose centre column is surmounted by Archangel Gabriel guarding the greatest figures of Hungary's thousand-year-old history. In front of the column, in the centre of the square, is the memorial to the heroes who fell for their country. On the right and left, closing the square, are two huge colonnaded buildings: the Museum of Fine Arts, housing a rich collection of Egyptian, Greek-Roman and European works of art, and the Art Gallery, the main exhibition hall for temporary shows of contemporary artists.
Behind the arcaded colonnade of the millen-

95

96

97

98

99

nial monument there is an open space. The surface of City Park Lake flashes before one's eyes, with the fortress-like museum of Vajdahunyad Castle on its shore. Behind it are the vast expanses of the City Park, with the adjacent Zoo and Amusement Park.
The whole complex appears to justify the planners, the men who dreamt of and realized a more perfect order for the city.

The "Inner City" of Pest

Buda has several centres, but none of them can be called an "inner city," just as the residential quarters in its surrounding hills cannot be called "garden suburbs".
On the left bank, however, the old nucleus of the city along the Danube—the Pest section between Margaret Bridge and Liberty Bridge—has preserved its status of an "inner city" to this day.
Here one finds the best—and most expensive—restaurants and cafés, as well as the best shops. There is no match in the rest of Pest for the row of hotels along the inner city section of the Danube bank. The principal administrative centre of the country, the Parliament, is also situated nearby. As a build-

100

101

102

100. *The Forum Hotel on the bank of the Danube*
101. *Café terrace in Kígyó Street...*
102. *...and a restaurant on the Danube corso*
103–107. *Open and closed spaces in the Inner City*
108 *The row of hotels by the Danube*

103

106

107

104

105

ing, it is a monumental mausoleum of the historic illusions of the former, long vanished and scattered Hungarian ruling classes. It is crowned with a multitude of spirelets, with a dome in the middle, and constitutes the largest single building complex on the river bank. In spite of this, its neo-Gothic structure makes it appear graceful. It is an apt symbol of the illusory world of the turn of the century, when it was fondly imagined that the greatness and power of the medieval Hungarian kingdom would survive the second millennium.

The Parliament turned out to be sumptous, if somewhat showy; but people got used to it and learned to live with it. "Since it turned out as it did, nothing can be done about it. We shall accept is as our own."

FORUM

110

111

The fact that the huge building complex does not dwarf any of the valuable historic buildings or monuments of the Inner City helps us excuse the Parliament its excesses. It cannot adversely affect its surroundings for its bulk is not wedged between other buildings. On one side it fronts the Danube, on the other the spacious Kossuth Lajos Square, named after the great leader of the Hungarian War of Independence. The two wings of the building are also surrounded by large open spaces.
The nearby (Liberty) Szabadság Square is also worthy of attention. Various Ministries, the National Bank, the Chamber of Commerce, the Television Centre, constitute a whole series of important public buildings.
The Inner City is studded with others, including the Hungarian Academy of Sciences, the Budapest Town Hall, the fine neo-classical building of the council of Pest County (i.e. the territory surrounding the capital), most Ministries, foreign trade companies and banks, and international airline companies; indeed, no other centre in the country is of similar importance.

109. *View of Parliament from Buda...*
110. *...and from Pest...*
111–112. *In part, and in whole*

112

However, even in this feverishly active centre, there are refuges for quiet contemplation. The centuries-old palace of Count Károlyi's family houses the Museum of Hungarian Literature, named after the 19th century revolutionary poet, Sándor Petőfi. One of the interesting buildings in Kossuth Square is the seat of the former Supreme Court which now houses the Ethnographical Museum. The romantic-style Vigadó or Redoute, now the Municipal Concert Hall, of which only a few smouldering ruins survived the devastation of the war, but

113

114

115

116

117

113. *The Gallery of Parliament*
114. *The grand staircase*
115. *The sixteen-pointed stars of the cupola*
116. *In a quiet corridor, statues recall the past*
117. *The Assembly Hall*

118

118–123. *Old statues in the Inner City*

121

119

120

122

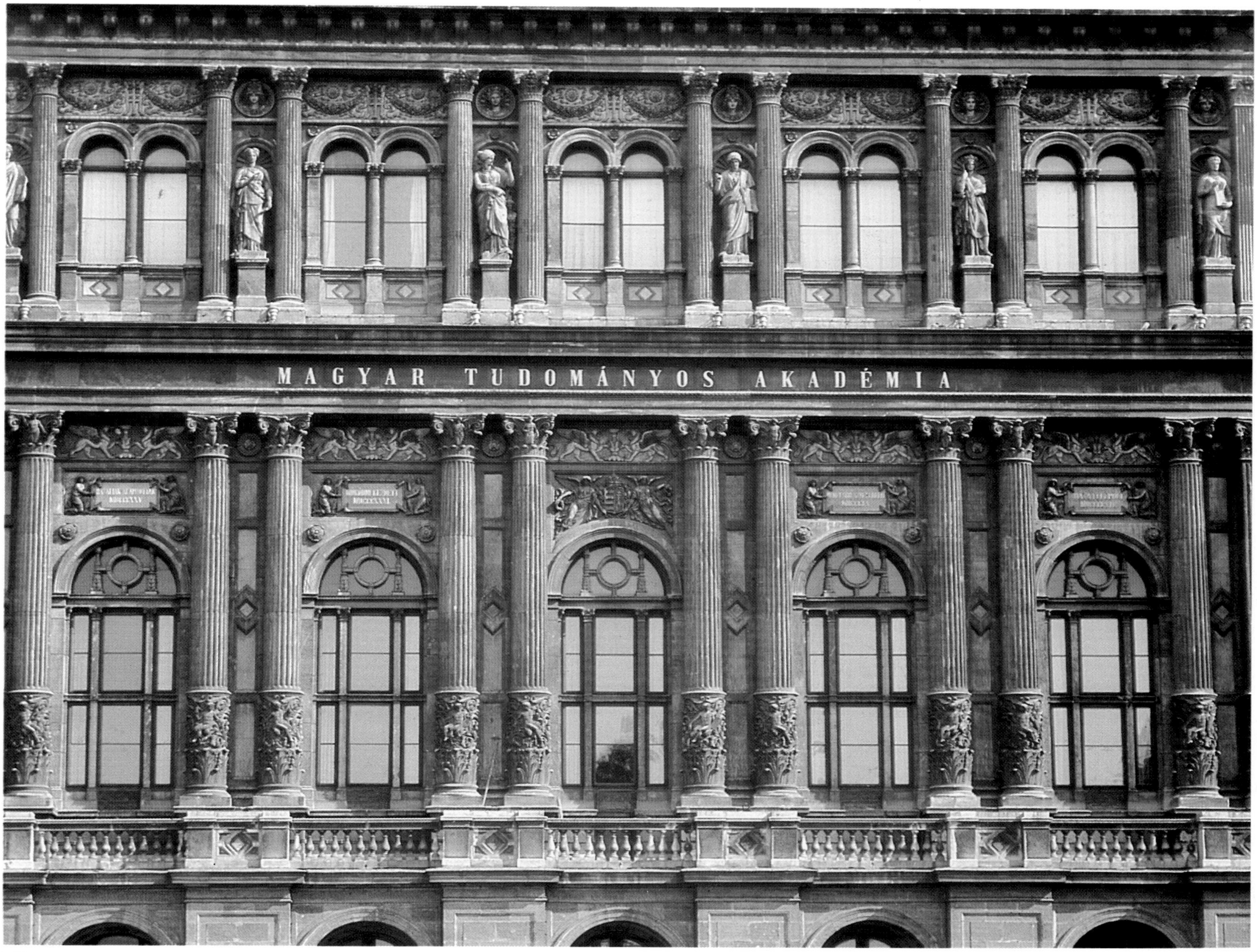

123

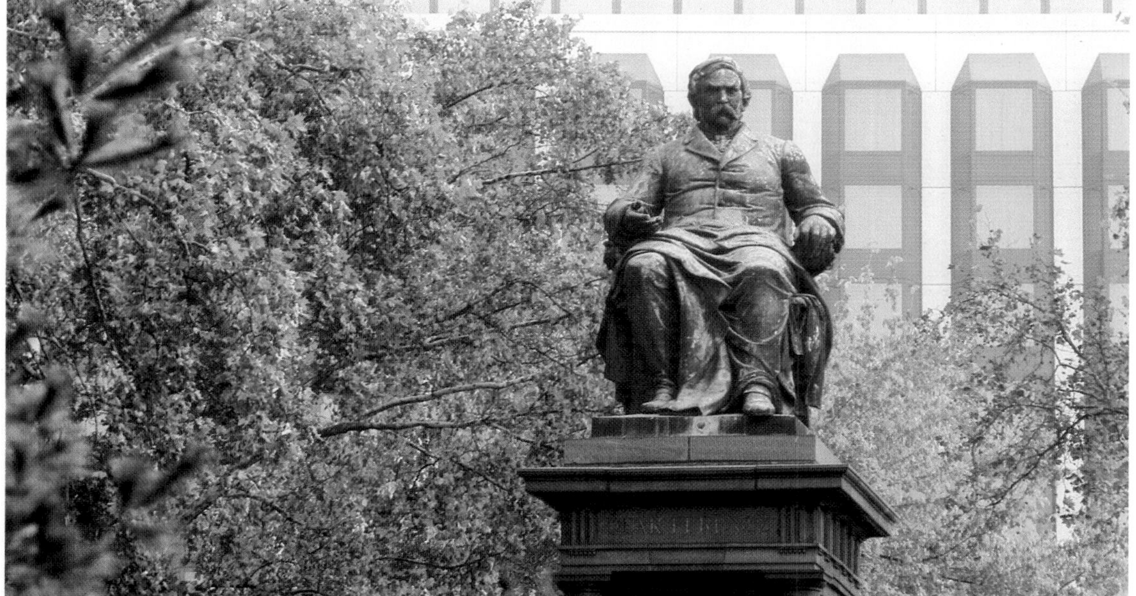

which has since been fully restored—is the scene of concerts, recitals and fine arts exhibitions.

Some of the churches of the Inner City also deserve mention. The oldest one stands on the river bank, at the Elizabeth Bridge. Part of its foundations are Roman ruins, part of its structure is built over its own remains, for the first version dating from Roman times was destroyed by Mongolian invaders in 1241–1242; later, the church was reconstructed in the Gothic style. Still later, Renaissance chancels were added to it, and during the period following, its façade was restored in the Baroque style. These historically different items fit together well. The only thing that may stick out is the small Turkish prayer-house attached to the southern wall of the chancel. It is indeed unusual in a Roman Catholic

↑ Ferenc Deák 1803–1876

124

126

127

124. *Romanticism and functionality (Vigadó Square)*
125. *The garden of the former Károlyi Mansion*
126. *The two Virgin Maries of Martinelli Square*
127–128. *Underpasses help speed traffic at Felszabadulás (Liberation) Square*

125

BIZTOSÍTÁS
PORCELÁN
MŰTÁRGY

129

129–133. *Felszabadulás Square and vicinity in the heart of the Inner City*
132. *Panorama of Pest from Gellért Hill*

church; yet it is not surprising if we bear in mind that for a century and a half (1541–1686) the church was used as a Mohammedan mosque.

The Baroque churches of the city also delight the eye. The finest among them are the University Church and the Franciscan Church. There are also two Greek Orthodox churches of interest, one Serbian and one Hungarian. Finally, in the Inner City stands St. Stephen's Basilica, the largest church in Hungary, named after the country's first Christian king. It was built in the mid-nineteenth century after several starts, because the dome collapsed while under construction. The front elevation of the huge building faces a relatively small square, but in spite of this it offers a fine view with the simple inscription above its doorway: EGO SUM VIA VERITAS ET VITA.

130

133

131

132

134

137

135

136

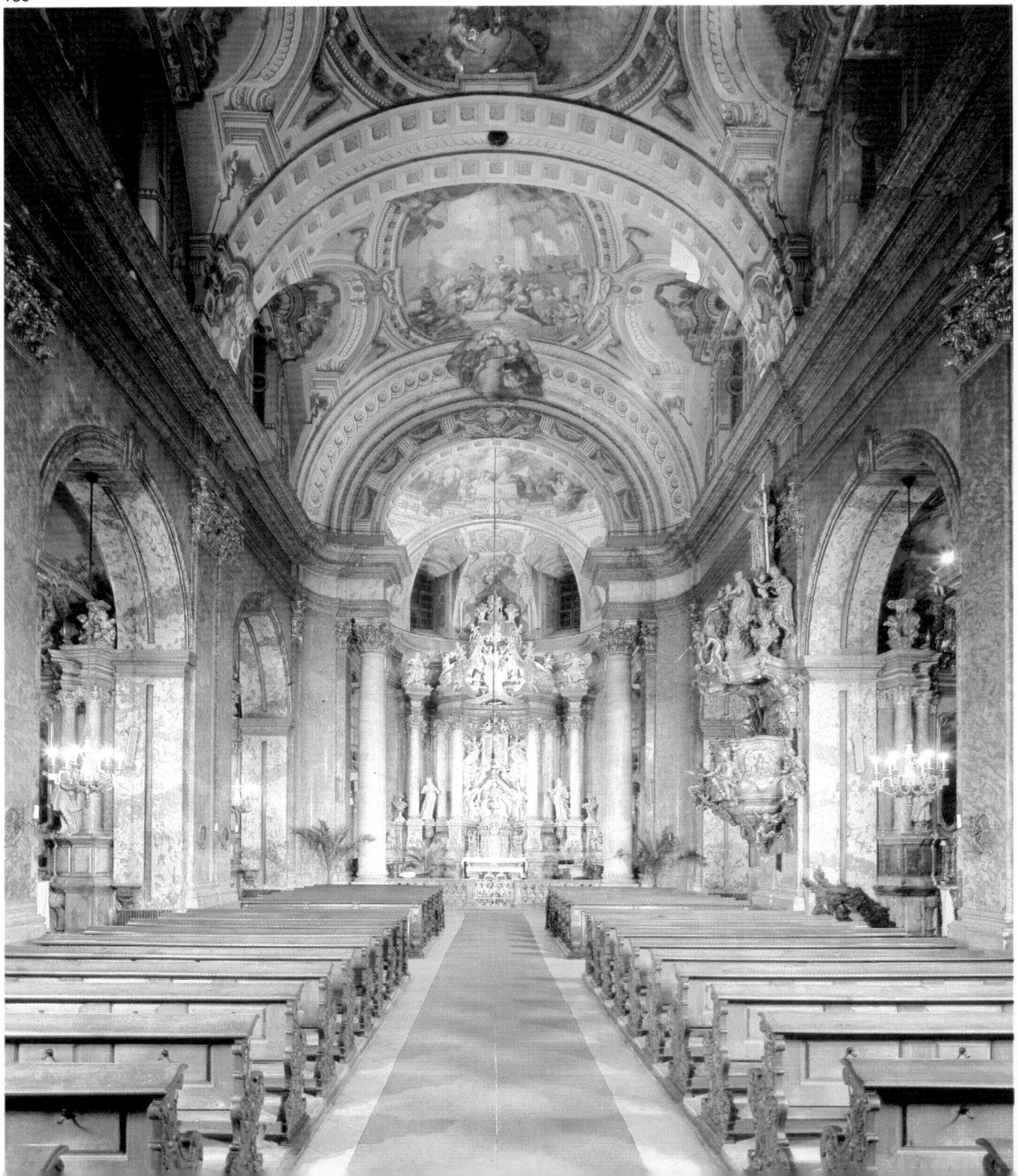

134. *Roman ruins near the Danube bank of Pest with the Inner City Parish Church in the background*
135. *Portal of the Catholic Church in Váci Street*
136–137. *University Church, one of the best examples of Baroque architecture in Pest*
138. *The Basilica*

138

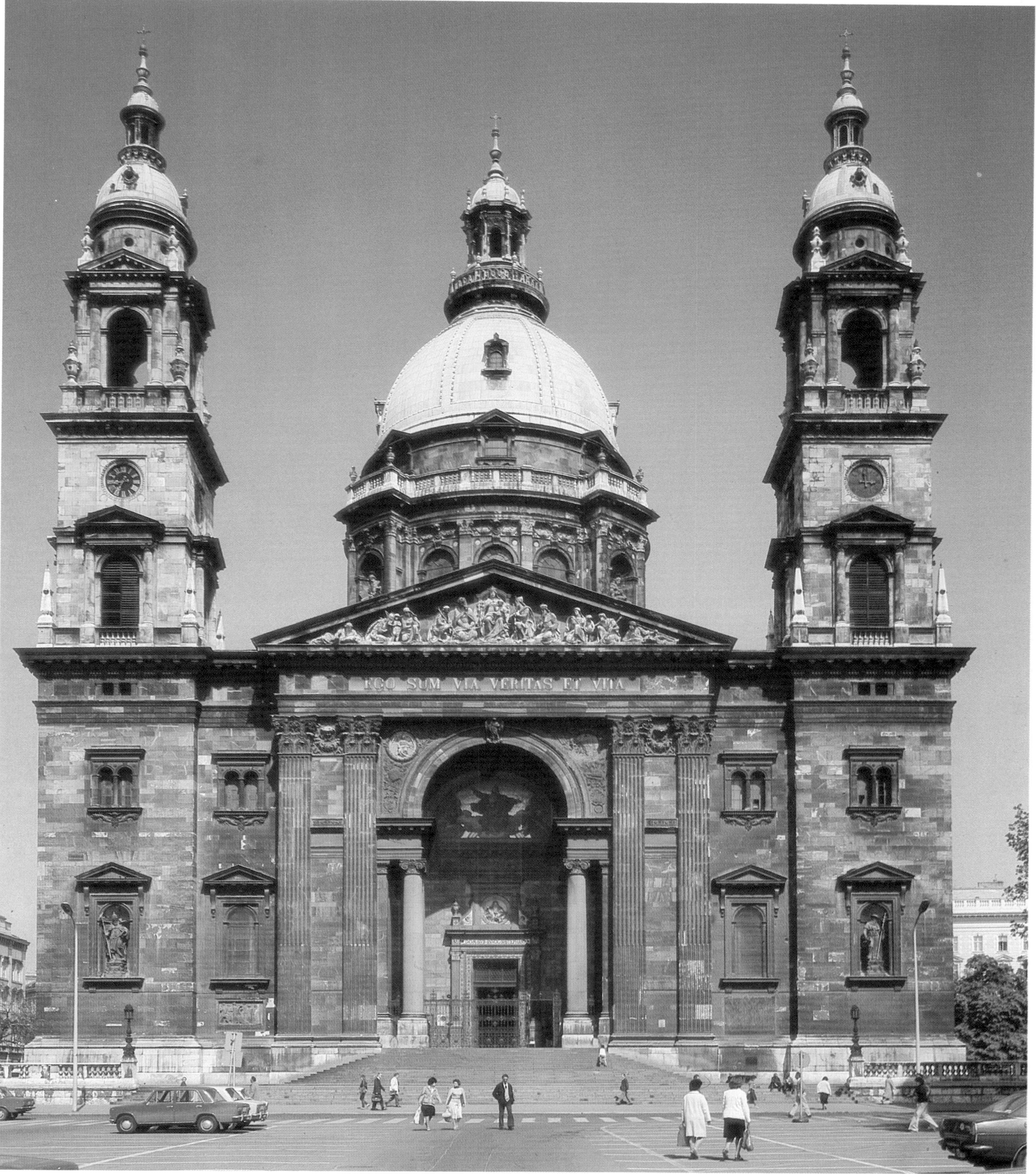

1851–1905

Where is Budapest?

Where exactly is Budapest, you may ask. One answer is: between Vienna and Belgrade. Its geographical co-ordinates are indicated by every map as latitude 47° 30′ north, and longitude 19° east. The same parallel passes through the city as goes through Bregenz in Austria, Winterthur in Switzerland, Angers in France and the north-western city of Seattle in the USA; and the same meridian as through Tromsö in Norway, Gungun in Zaire and Worcester in South Africa.
Still, these data tell us little about Budapest, except that it is situated a little nearer to the North Pole than to the equator, and that the clocks run on Central European time, which means that they are one hour ahead of GMT. However these positional aspects reveal little of the city's geographical and historical situation which so influenced its development. It will help to convey a clearer picture if we say that Budapest is one of the metropolises of East-Central Europe. It belongs to Central Europe, however, even if situated in its eastern part.
For us, today, Central Europe appears to have become overshadowed. The East-West political division of the Continent makes many people forget that the existence of Central Europe as such is a thousand-year-old fact of history.
This is confirmed also by Budapest. From its history, we may learn of the past of a city first founded within the Roman Empire, in the province known as Pannonia, before the birth of Christ, of a past which in the Middle Ages tied the fate of the city to that of Rome

139

140

141

142

139. *Ruins of a Roman amphitheatre in Óbuda*
140–142. *Gothic stone cornice . . . Turkish cupola . . . Baroque patron saint of the city, in stone*
143, 146. *Neo-Classical façade of the former County Hall and the* turul *bird of the Castle, a product of Neo Romanticism at the time of the Millennium*
144, 145, 147. *The Rococo in Buda, Eclecticism and Art Nouveau in Pest*

144

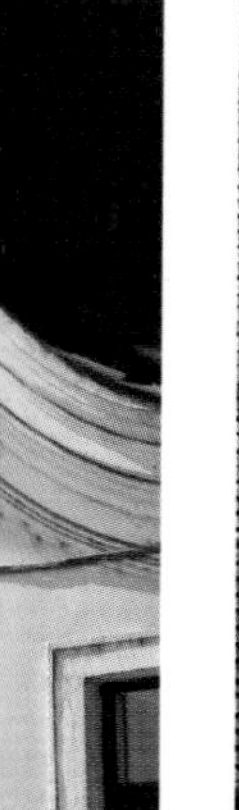

147

145

rather than Byzantium, of a past which did not seal off Hungary from the well-springs of the Roman, Gothic and Renaissance spirit and art. True, the century and a half of Turkish rule (1541—1686) caused a considerable break in its development, and the wars connected with the occupation destroyed much of what had previously been created here by the spirit and art of the West. However, some of the surviving Turkish remains add here and there special colour to the city. The eighteenth- and nineteenth-century buildings reveal the prevalence of Western influence with the Baroque, Rococco and Louis XVI styles and the later local versions of Neo-Classical and Romantic art. Hungary, and in particular Pest-Buda, were never excluded from any new or important trend in Europe, even *Sezession,* the special Austrian and Eastern European version of Art Nouveau, or the "pure formalism" of the architecture which followed.

Ruins along the limes

From Asia Minor to Britain, the Roman Empire left quantities of ruins behind. In Budapest the remains of the ancient border defences, the *limes* of Pest, are clearly discernible even today.

It is evident that the *limes* was not a kind of ancient Maginot Line dug in the earth and filled with defensive engines. The borders of the Empire were defended by a long chain of watch-towers, forts and military camps. They were connected with each other, as well as with the back areas, by excellent roads.

Most of the permanent military camps lived

their own lives as individual settlements, often in symbiosis with the civilian towns established next to them. This is how it was in Óbuda, the northern part of present-day Buda. The twin towns of Aquincum lived together but never fully merged into each other. They even had their separate circus shows. The inhabitants of the military camp had an amphitheatre accommodating 14,000 people, while the civilian population went to another seating about 6,000. The upper tiers of what remained of these amphitheatres were carried off piecemeal by later housebuilders; but the lower tiers and underground chambers which housed the wild beasts, actors and gladiators, can still be seen.

The guarding of the Pannonian *limes* was fortunately greatly facilitated by the Danube. However, to protect the crossing points on both sides of the river, the Romans built scattered fortifications on the left bank as well. This is how Transaquincum and later Contra-Aquincum became established in the second century, A. D. Ruins of later fortifications have been excavated next to the Elizabeth Bridge in Pest.

There are naturally many more archaeolgical remains on the Buda side of the river. The most extensive excavations have been carried

149

148

150

151

152

153

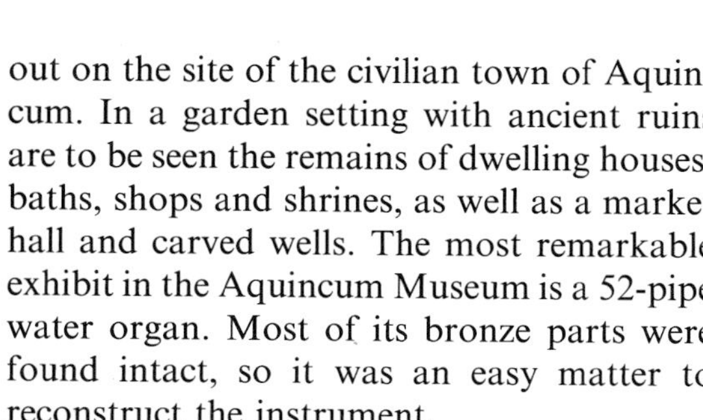

out on the site of the civilian town of Aquincum. In a garden setting with ancient ruins are to be seen the remains of dwelling houses, baths, shops and shrines, as well as a market hall and carved wells. The most remarkable exhibit in the Aquincum Museum is a 52-pipe water organ. Most of its bronze parts were found intact, so it was an easy matter to reconstruct the instrument.

Many a grave and grave-stone were also found in Aquincum. The archaeologists also encountered a trefoil-shaped old Christian graveyard chapel known as the *cella trichora,* while several Mithraic shrines proclaim widespread veneration of the Old-Persian Sun god, which must have been introduced by soldiers sent here from Syria.

In the military town, a public bath with several pools, a steam room and central heating system remained comparatively intact. The waters of the thermal springs of Buda were also conducted to this bath.

The inhabitants of Aquincum bathed at the small island formerly situated at the upper end of Margaret Island, where abundant natural thermal springs gushed forth. However, the Danube gradually washed away the island, carrying with it the ruins of the Roman baths as well.

148. *The Roman ruins of Aquincum, former headquarters of Lower Pannonia*
149. *Roman mosaic in Buda (Meggyfa Street)*
150–152. *Finds from the Roman Empire in the Open-Air Museum of Aquincum*
153. *Roman capital among the prefabricated apartment houses of Óbuda*
154. *The gentle, southern slope of Castle Hill seen from Gellért Hill*

155

155–159. *Gothic faces and figures from the court of Sigismund of Luxemburg (1368–1437). Some examples of the fabulous 1974 find in the Budapest Historical Museum*
156. *Knightly tournament on a medieval stove tile*

157

156

An underground kingdom

Cities do not move about, at least not in space. Perhaps in time. But time also changes the space surrounding them. Transferred political boundaries and economic lines of force may easily change their destiny.

At the time of the fall of the Western Roman Empire in the fifth century, the mid-Danube *limes* ceased to exist. So did the urban life of the region. Only a heap of ruins remained on the site of one-time Aquincum. Huns, Goths, Avars and other mounted warrior peoples of the East brought their herds to graze this side of and beyond the Danube.

A decisive change took place around the year A. D. 1000, when our ancestors, the Magyars, who settled in the Carpathian Basin, were converted—at almost the same time as the Bohemians and Poles—to Christianity, and these three Roman Catholic kingdoms established east of Germany entered on a course of European development. Soon urbanization commenced all over the Continent, giving rise to Óbuda in place of Aquincum, while Pest gradually developed on the opposite bank of the Danube. Not much later

160. *Knight and his herald: reconstruction of a Gothic statue in the Fehérvár Rondella*

158

159

Buda also began to grow as the southern neighbour of Óbuda.

At the end of the Middle Ages, these three cities formed the centre of a feudal Hungarian state extending throughout the Carpathian Basin, only to find themselves again in a peripheral position when the conquering Turkish Empire incorporated them—overnight, as it were—as European border cities of a small province under military government, with the Pasha of Buda at its head.

The Turkish occupation and the final siege, launched by united European armies to drive the Turks out in 1686, reduced the splendid medieval Hungarian royal palaces to mere ruins.

Yet, visitors to Buda Castle can project themselves into the past centuries when Buda was still ruled by Hungarian kings.

Having annexed Hungary to their empire, the Habsburgs replaced the destroyed medieval palace in Buda with a castle. This eighteenth and nineteenth-century building, incorporating parts of the ancient castle walls and bastions, had to be reconstructed again after the Second World War. From the Castle as it stands today, long flights of steps lead down

160

161

162

161. *Reconstructed medieval fortifications on the southern side of Castle Hill*
162. *Towers of the Lihegő Gate and the Great Southern Bastion*
163. *Bastion of Veli Bey with the memorial to the Transylvanian Hussar Regiment of the First World War*
164. *Part of the western Castle wall*

163

164

to halls and vaults of medieval origin. Numerous relics of the long-vanished medieval rous relics of the long-vanished medieval Hungarian kingdom are preserved here, most notably survivals—even if in ruins or fragments—from the palaces which once stood on this site.

In the large Gothic hall dating from around 1420 and the similarly-styled Gothic undercroft can be seen special medieval art treasures: a series of stone statues of kings, knights, ladies, and saints. According to all available evidence, they were carved in the time of Sigismund of Luxembourg, King of Hungary and Holy Roman Emperor (1387–1437). They were probably buried underground as superfluous rubbish some time in the mid-fifteenth century. Many of them were found smashed to pieces, but those which remained intact or whose fragments could be successfully assembled—after the excavation of this cemetery of sculpture in 1974—powerfully evoke the European atmosphere of nearly six-hundred years ago.

Stone carvings of somewhat later date, recalling the splendour of the Renaissance palace of Matthias Corvinus (1458–1490), are also worthy of attention. Most of them are of

165. *Silver gilt flask of Matthias Corvinus (c. 1443–1490)*
166. *White marble Renaissance portrait of Queen Beatrice (1457–1508)*
167. *Pedestal of the gold Matthias Calvary*

165

166

167

Hungarian red marble; but the relief carved in 1489 representing the royal couple is of Italian white marble.
Writing about King Matthias, Antonio Bonfini, the Italian humanist author said:

"On the front overlooking the Danube, he [the King] had a chapel built. This he provided with a water-organ and a double font made of marble and silver. Higher up he had a library built which he filled with a rich collection of books, sumptuous even in their covers. South from this, there is a vaulted hall, the ceiling of which shows the whole firmament . . . There are some spacious dining halls and superb bed-chambers. The door-frames are embellished with marquetry. The decorative fire-places are surmounted by quadrigas and other Roman-style ornaments. Below is the treasury with other store-rooms and an armoury."

And so he continues with his description. However, not long after the Turkish invasion all of this was destroyed. Part of it was buried underground, other parts still deeper, in oblivion.

168

169

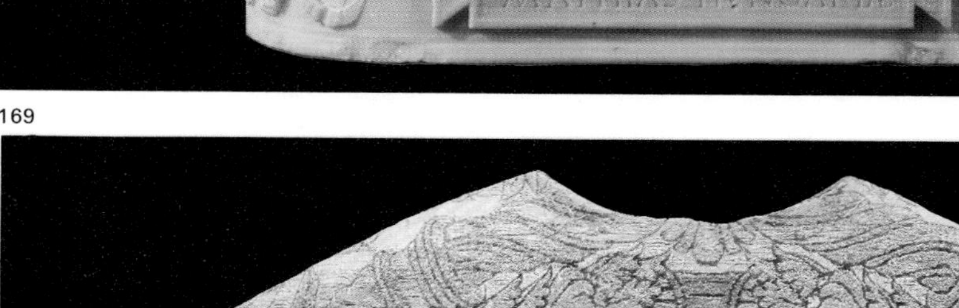

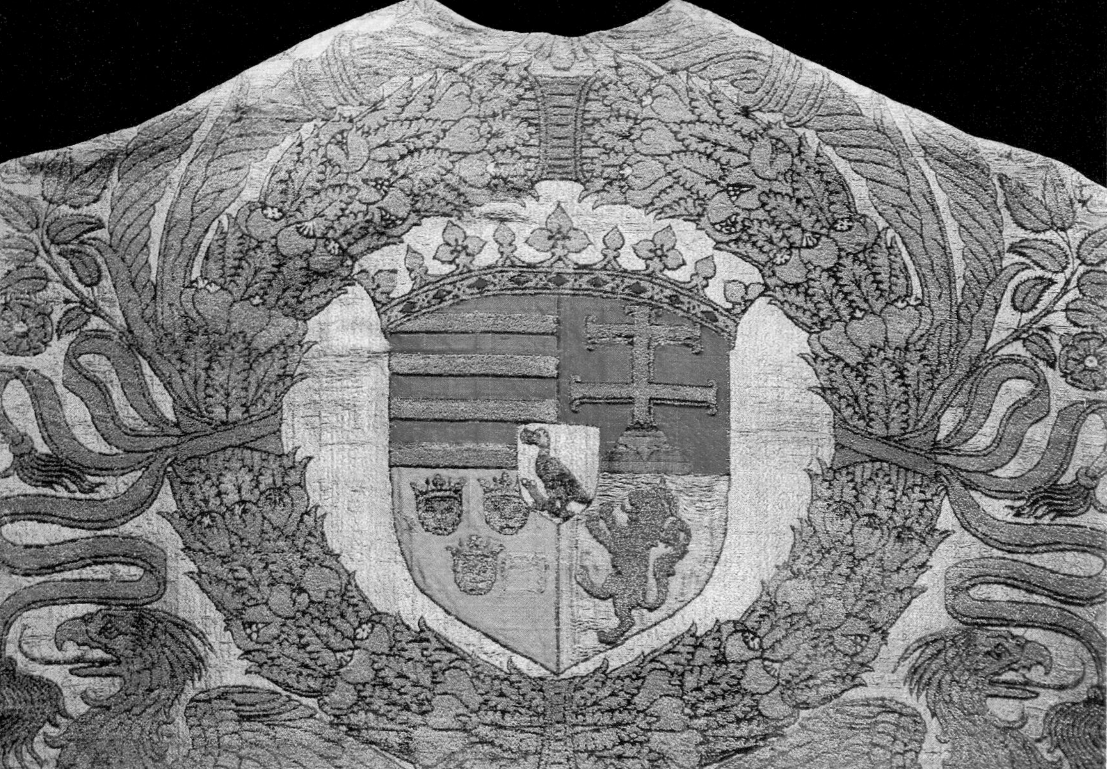

168. *Portrait of King Matthias*
169. *Upholstery of King Matthias's throne with his coat of arms*
170. *Medieval stove tile with the figure of King Matthias*
171. *The Castle District*

170

The burghers of Buda

Wherever imperial or royal castles were built on hill-tops in Europe, towns for burghers were generally established at their foot. Castle Hill in Buda was, however, large enough to be shared by both the court and the civil inhabitants of the town.

The Royal Castle complex was naturally somewhat more spread out than the ordinary houses which are situated close to each other to this day. However, the streets of the town were never so narrow that the drivers of carriages proceeding in opposite directions or rumbling past each other would have come into collision.

The old inhabitants of the houses in Buda generally engaged in some farming, in addition to pursuing their chosen trade. They gathered in the harvest from their vineyards on the surrounding hills, just as they cropped the hay required for their animals.

Carts with their loads had plenty of room under the archways of the houses. In the side-walls of the narrow archways were rows

172

172. *The Mace Tower*
173–175. *Gates in the Castle District*
176. *Gothic sedilia behind the portal at No. 32 Úri Street*

173

175

174

176

of so-called *sedilia,* whose purpose has not been clarified to this day.

Many of the *sedilia* are still extant, mainly because far fewer houses were buried during the Turkish conquest than were royal buildings. Most of them were left damaged but not completely ruined after the expulsion of the Turks. Part of the walls were still standing and their strong foundations also survived. The restorers made use of these, incorporating the ruins into their new Baroque style houses.

The *sedilia* and Gothic windows were walled in, of course. The devastation of the Second World War was responsible for revealing from under the fallen plaster fragments of medieval Buda.

177

177. *The National Archives at the northern end of the Castle District*

178. *Statue of Pallas Athene with the coat of arms of Buda on the corner of the former Town Hall of Buda*

179. *"Floating" female figure of a Classicist appartment house on the corner of Ország-ház Street and Petermann bíró Street*

180. *Bay window of the former Town Hall of Buda*

181. *Where Táncsics Mihály Street runs into Bécsi Kapu Square*

178

179

180

181

182

183

Often these fragments were of considerable dimensions. There are a number of houses on Castle Hill which freed from their later extensions, plaster cornices and mortar surfaces, have regained, either fully or partly, their fourteenth-, fifteenth- and sixteenth-century form in the course of restorations following the Second World War.

The restorations involved a tremendous amount of work, for in 1945 the Castle District lay in ruins. It had already suffered earlier devastation under the Turks, as a result of which it lost its original aspect. So experts tried to restore every house in its original ancient form, though only in so far as they could follow surviving architectural elements. They always observed the strict requirements of authenticity, relying not on imagination but information gathered from the walls and stones wherever possible. They uncovered every part of the ancient houses down to the last cornerstone, and their subsequent work was determined by their findings. Thus the Castle District was reborn. It became—in spite of the previous devastation—even more "ancient" and beautiful than it had been before the Second World War.

The Gothic and Renaissance past of the district has acquired greater emphasis, as did the medieval and Turkish elements of the fortifications. Yet this emphasis is not out of proportion, and does not disrupt the basically Baroque atmosphere of the Castle District.

Sometimes, the late evening hour or a summer night seems to conjure up the ancient aspect of Buda in the minds of people stroll-

184

186

185

187

182. *Fortuna Street and Táncsics Mihály Street begin at Bécsi Kapu Square* [handwritten: At the other (southern) end at Hess András Square]
183. *Old gate in Országház Street*
184. *Bay-window of the house at No. 5 Bécsi Kapu Square*
185. *Houses on Fortuna Street* [handwritten: Looking south from Bécsi Kapu Square]
186. *Early Neo-Classic apartment houses on Bécsi Kapu Square*
187. *Window on Bécsi Kapu Square*

The Red Hedgehog, A Vörös Sün
#3 Hess András Square

188

189

191

192

190

193

ing along its streets. Let us cite here Gyula Krúdy, the great Hungarian Impressionist writer of the beginning of the century, who wrote in one of his novels:

"Mr. Rezeda lived in Buda in the Castle District; walking home at night, he often met kings who stepped out of the stone walls. Rezeda politely lifted his hat before Matthias, who wore a student's gown, or before the grim figure of black-bearded Sigismund; he would remain standing beside the bastion with head bent until the phantoms of the kings—composed of the mist of autumnal nights, the silver of the pale moon, and dully echoing ringing of bells

194

195

188–193. Façade and corner decorations on the old houses of the Castle District
194. *Baroque fresco on the façade at No. 16 Táncsics Mihály Street*
195. *Façade of the house No. 10 in Táncsics Mihály Street*
196. *Café in Fortuna Street*
197. *Medieval commercial building with characteristic second level which juts out at No. 14 Tárnok Street*

196

197

198–202. *Gates and yards at No. 16 Táncsics Mihály Street, No. 25 Fortuna Street, at No. 16 Országház Street and No. 31 Úri Street*

198

199

200

201

202

in ancient towers—disappeared again somewhere along the Castle walls. On other occasions he stopped in one of the deeply slumbering streets to listen to the sounds of revelry that he fancied came from underground, from cellars and vaulted tunnels under the Castle. Who knows which king's brave warriors had been left behind in the cellars under the Castle because of their drinking bouts . . .? Then, ladies of the Court, enveloped in cloaks, stole past him in the silent night with steps as noiseless as the wind in a grareyard. Some of them had golden heels on their little shoes. The wings of their cloaks touched Mr. Rezeda's shoulders" . . .

Such fantasies, however, require the dead of night. Kings? Soldiers? Ladies? In day-time,

203–204. *Wrought iron flag holder and old gate in Fortuna Street*
205. *Row of windows at No. 16 Táncsics Mihály Street*
206. *Old dwelling houses in Táncsics Mihály Street*

203

204

205

206

it is the recollection of substantial tradesmen and craftsmen that best suits the streets, mews, archways and courtyards, whether they date back two, four or five hundred years.

The ancient citizens were Germans, Hungarians and Jews. The latter lived in what is today's Táncsics Mihály utca, called Jew Street at that time. To posterity they left two medieval synagogues and some ancient tombstones. Excavated Jewish relics are at present in a special small museum.

The Germans and Hungarians had their separate churches. The German one, originally called the Church of Our Lady, is at present known as the Matthias Church. Under Turkish rule it was converted into a great

(207) → FOTO # 170 THIS HOUSE HAS SEDILLA → FOTO # 176

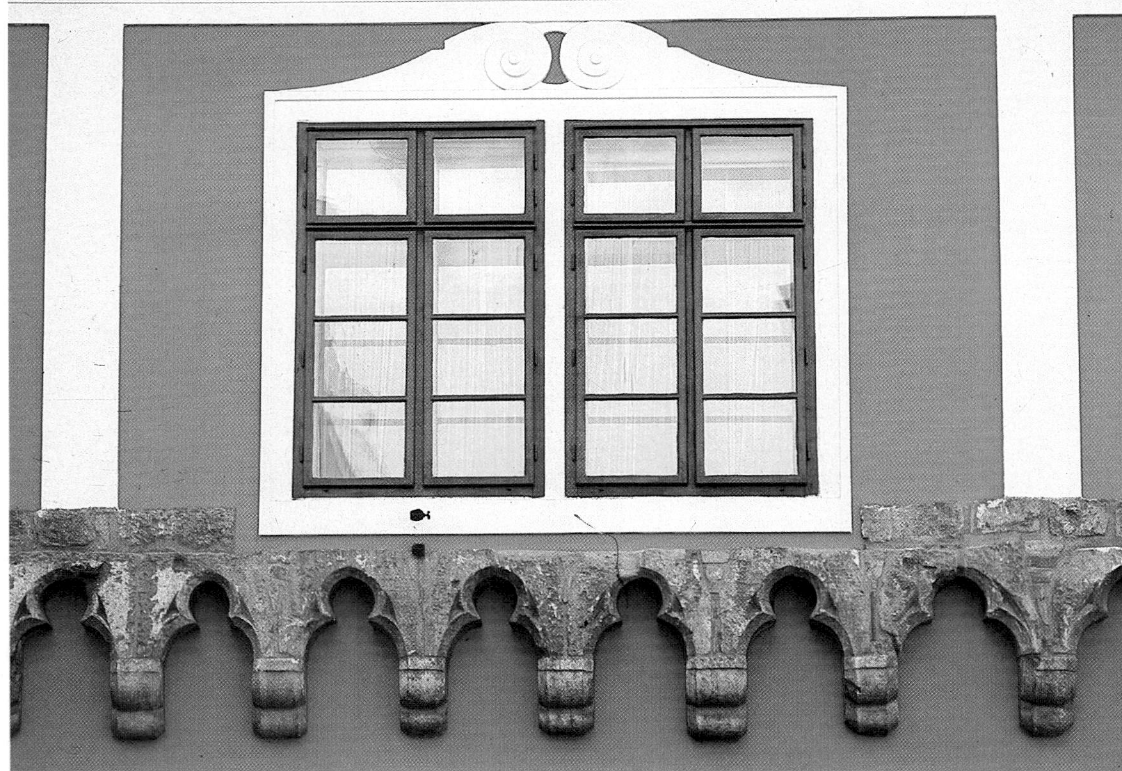

208

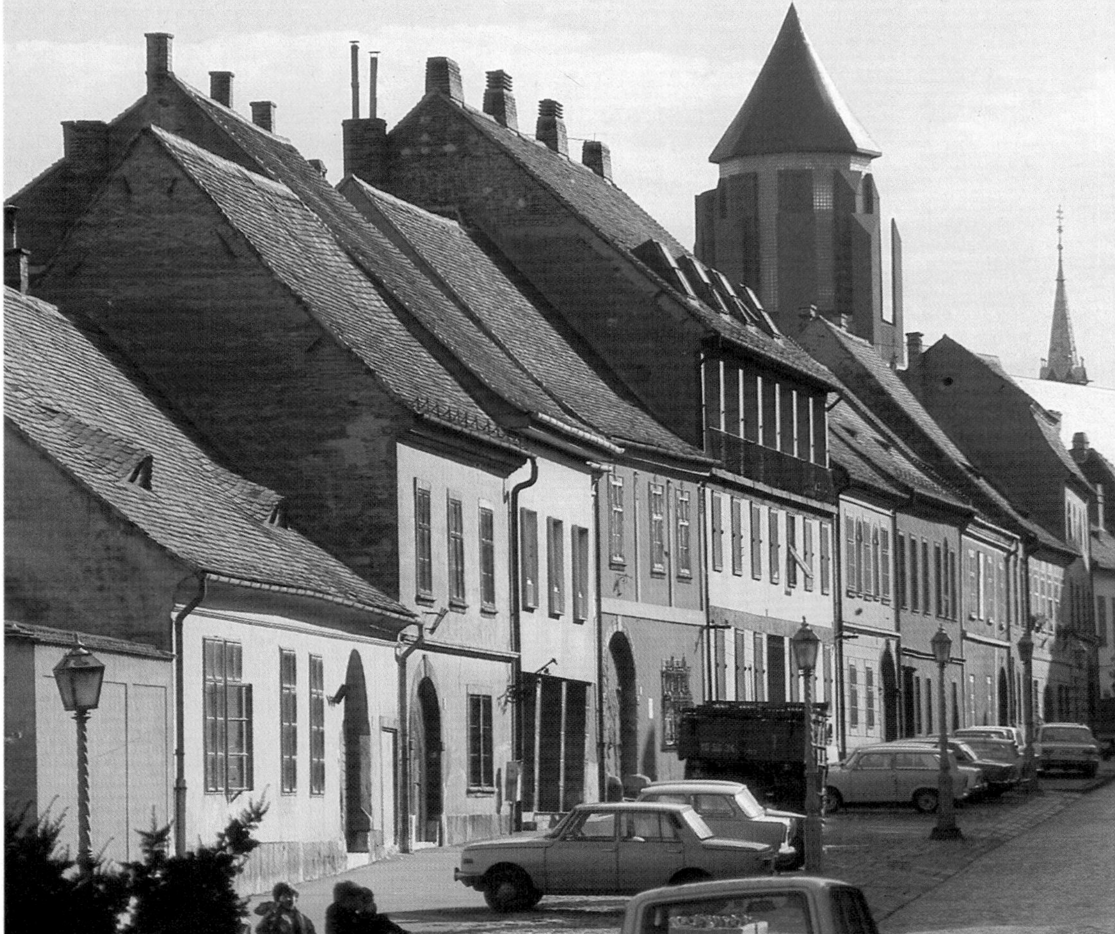

207. *Medieval carved stone cornice at No. 20 Országház Street*
208. *Fortuna Street* - LOOKING SOUTH
E/S

209. *Baroque coat of arms on the façade of a mansion at No. 58 in Úri Street*
210–211. *Old maple-wood gate of the same mansion*
212. *The former Town Hall of Buda on Szentháromság Square*

209

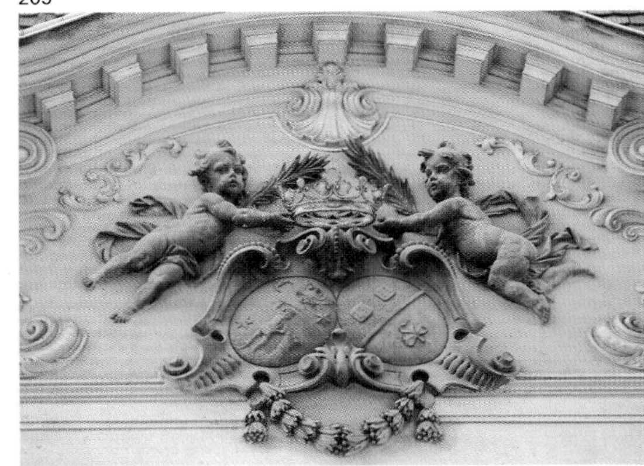

210

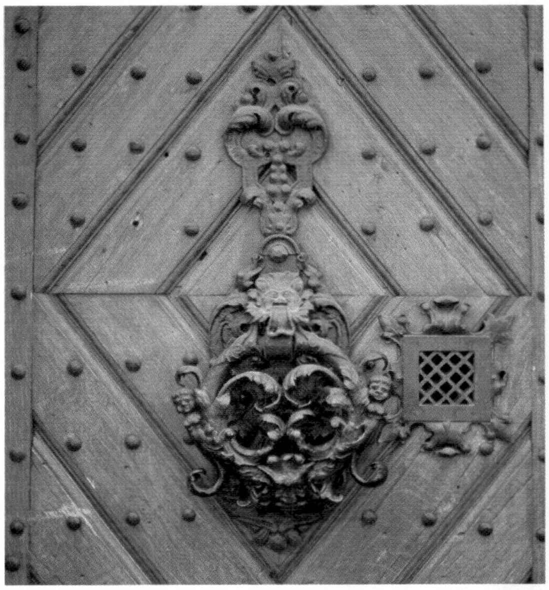

211

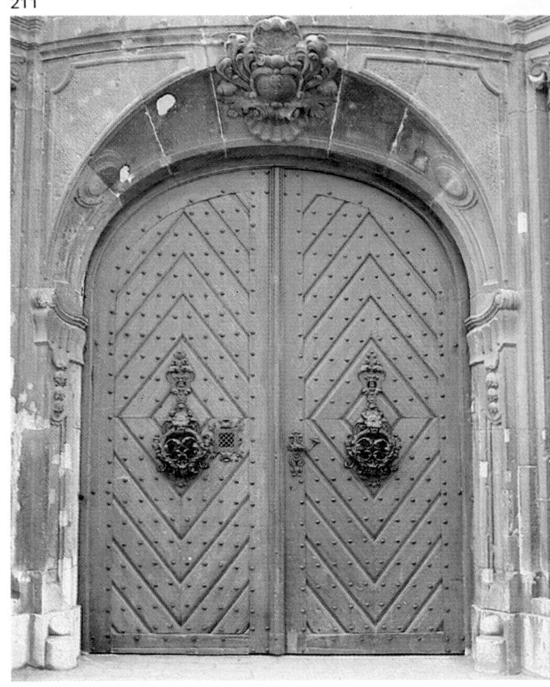

#7

213. *The famous Ruszwurm Confectionery in Szentháromság Street* Since 1827 !!
214. *One of the towers of the Matthias Church*
215. *Baroque and Neo-Gothic: the Trinity Statue and Matthias Church*
216. *A new statue and building on Szentháromság Square*
217. *Matthias Church seen from the park below Fishermen's Bastion*

214

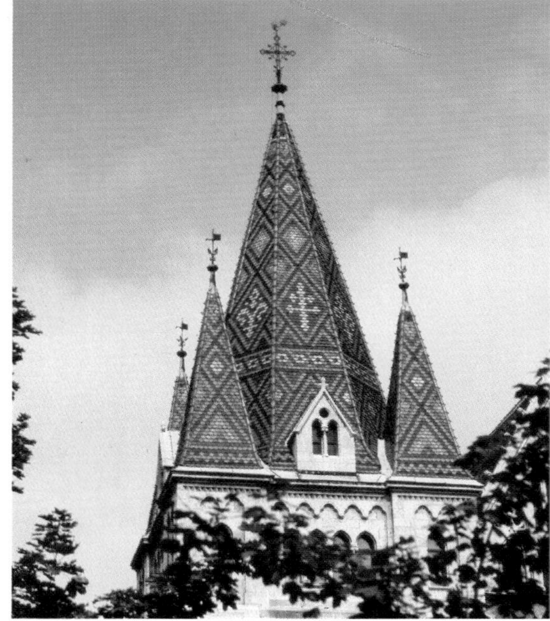

215

213) Was a Gingerbread Shop in the Middle Ages.

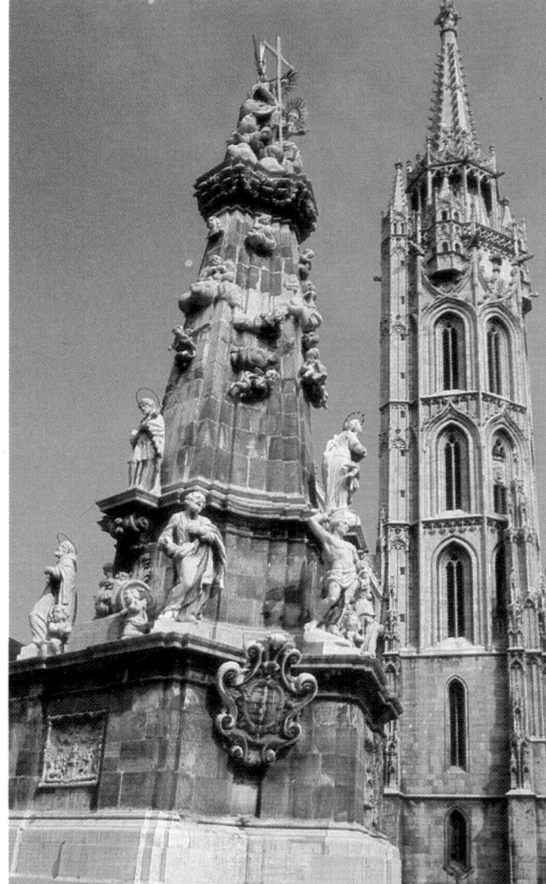

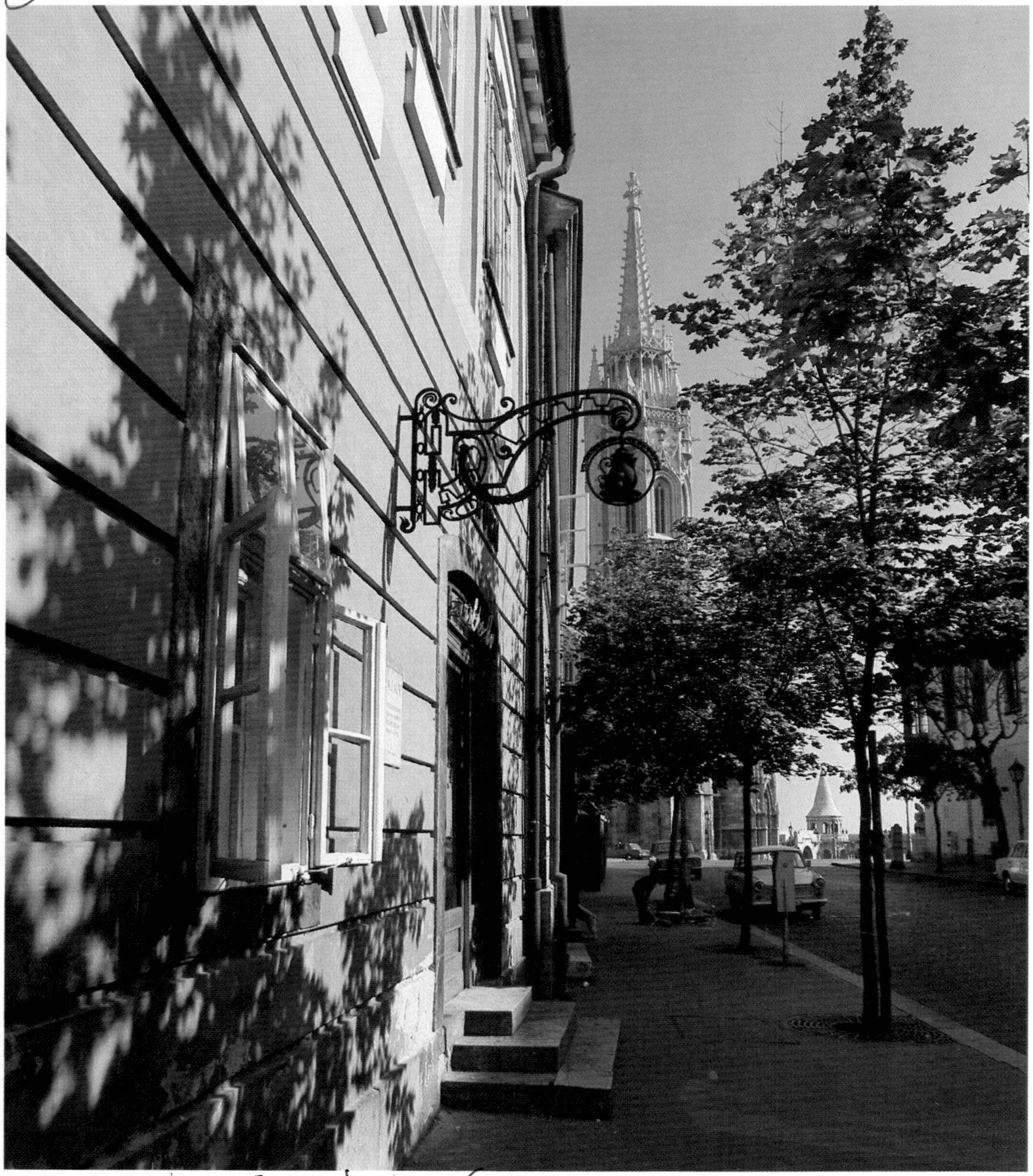

N/S of Street Looking East

216

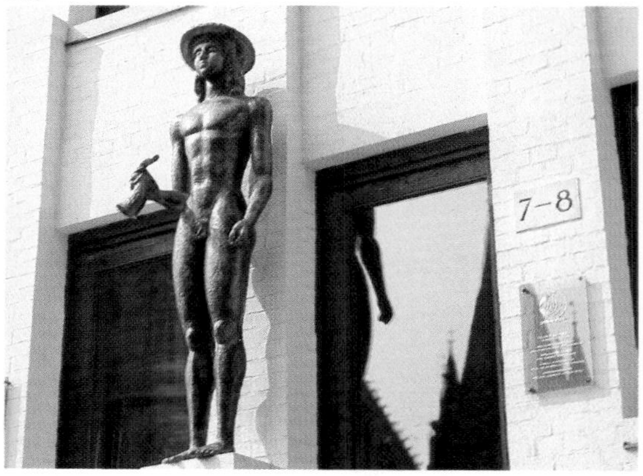

mosque or *djami;* later it was restored in Baroque style; only at the end of the past century did it regain, through repeated restoration, if not exactly an identical, yet a very similar appearance to the original Gothic building. There was also a Hungarian Church dedicated to Mary Magdalene, which was likewise reconstructed in the Baroque style. Visitors to the Castle may find some recompense for this loss in the Gothic remains incorporated in the Hilton Hotel complex, some of them only recently uncovered. Something quite unusual happened in this connection in the 1970s. The modern hotel was built in the immediate vicinity of Matthias Church, on a site where previously the remains of a medieval Dominican monastery dedicated to

217

218

219

220

218–220. Matthias Church
221. The sanctuary
222. The southern gate
223. Sitting figure of King Matthias built in the side wall of the medieval Nicholas Tower
224. The Hilton, built behind Baroque walls
225. The espresso terrace of the Hilton

221

222

225

St. Nicholas stood, together with the monastic church and a later Baroque building. The new building construction not only spared all the historic remains but organically attached them to the hotel. Open-air concerts today are held within the walls of the ruined church; the former cloisters, with an original carved stone fountain, were incorporated into the hotel premises. The Baroque building also serves the hotel's purposes, as does the medieval tower next to it, the western wall of which shows the seated figure of King Matthias. This carved stone relief is an authentic copy of the contemporary work produced in Bautzen (Silesia).

The word "copy" may have a disillusioning

224

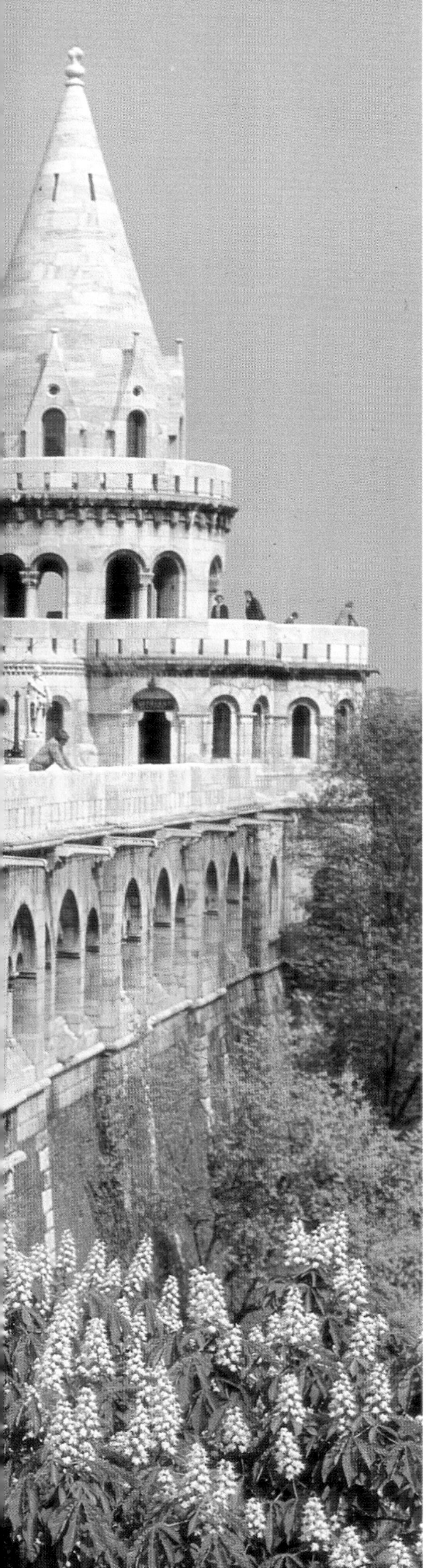

227

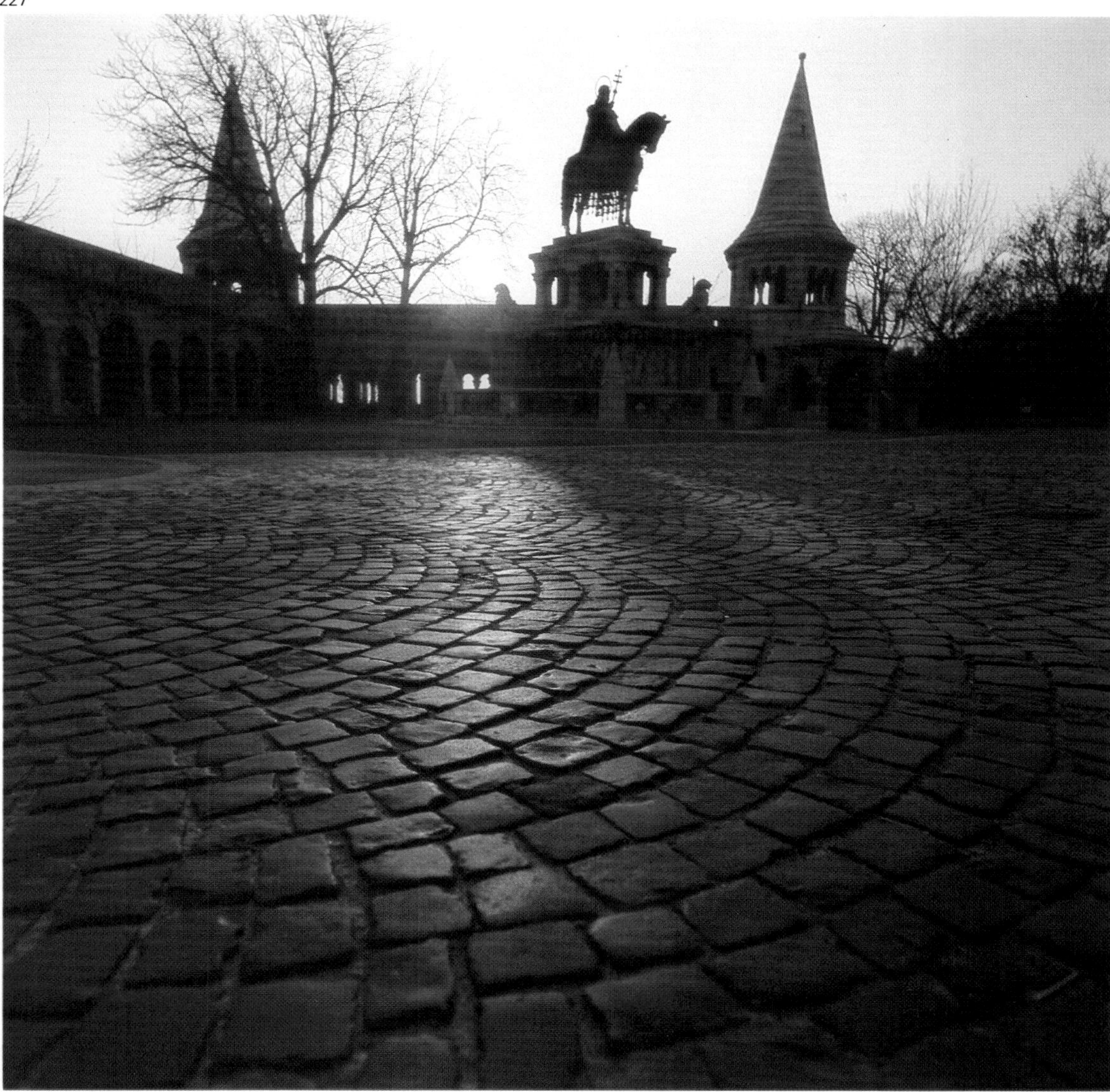

effect on the visitor. However, it is better not to deceive ourselves. It must be borne in mind that the followers of Mahomet did not tolerate the representation of the human form in their country, except on miniatures. Matthias himself had an original fifteenth-century statue in Buda which, however, showed a standing figure, not a seated one. The King had it cast in metal, similar to the statue of his father, János Hunyadi, whose victory in 1456 against the Turks at Nándorfehérvár (now Belgrade) is commemorated by the ringing of church bells at noon all over the world. The King had a further statue cast of his brother László, whom the young and jealous Habsburg ruler, Ladislas V, beheaded only a few months after the triumph at Belgrade (1) which had saved the country from Turkish invasion. All this belongs to the past, and it was a matter of course that it had to perish when Buda became Budin, a border town and jealously guarded stronghold, an advanced base of the Turkish Empire in Europe.

(1) i.e. NÁNDORFEHÉRVÁR
1456, JÁNOS HUNYADI

226. *Neo-Romanesque towers and terraces of the Fishermen's Bastion*
227. *The Bastion with the statue of St. Stephen*
228. *One of the staircases of the Bastion*

228

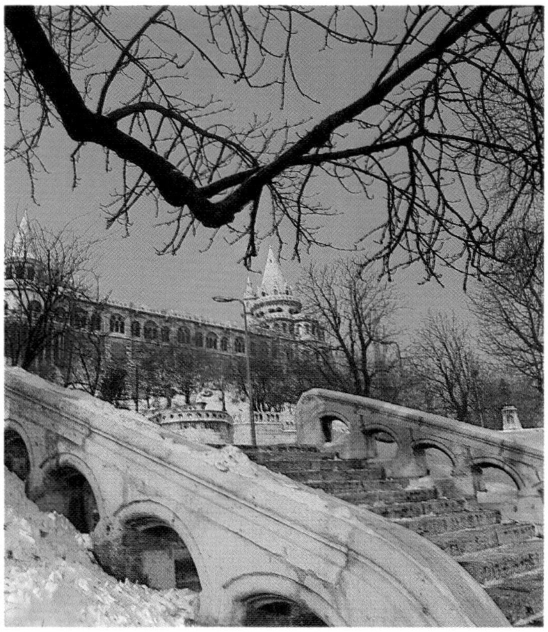

229

229. *Turkish "turbaned" tombstones on the side of Castle Hill*
230. *Memorial plaque to Kassim Pasha on the wall of the bastion he had built*
231. *Turkish cupolas of the Király Baths in Watertown*

The Crescent Moon over the town

The Turks of today hardly understand why their ancestors evoke so many bad memories in Hungary. They like the Hungarians, and always have. They harboured the Hungarian freedom-fighters Thököly, Rákóczi, Kossuth together with their followers, protecting them against the Habsburgs. Thus they sincerely deplore when—of all nationalities—Hungarians consider them barbarians, devastators and enemies who ruined their country. Sultan Suleiman II and his successors did not come to Hungary to lay waste the land. They came to conquer in the name of the Prophet, under the green flag of Allah, to win or to die. Hungary was destined to be the scene of a hundred- and- fifty years of war between the great Islamic Empire of the Turks and Christian Europe. Here ran the front-line, moving back and forth. It was here that enemies had to cause as much damage as they could, not only to a country's forces but also to her castles, towns and villages. It was regarded heroic not merely to defeat but to weaken the other: to burn, devastate and plunder on the other side of the front. And of course, to kill, murder and even drive away the surviving inhabitants.

According to certain historians, the whole period of Turkish rule did not damage Hungary as much as the war of liberation in the 1680s. In 1686, after a siege lasting several months, the Castle of Buda fell to the united Christian armies as a mere heap of ruins. The town was also in ruins, as was the former Royal Palace, that is to say, the historic buildings of Hungary, as well as those dating from

230

Turkish times. Of the latter, only some bastions survive here and there.

For the record, let us add that of the twelve *djamis* in Buda, one actually survived the siege of 1686 and one stood in Pest for some time after that date. Religious intolerance was evidently responsible for their later disappearance. It was not during the war, but in the peaceful eighteenth century, that they vanished.

Fortunately, bathing was not a thing prohibited by the Christian faith, even though it did not enjoin it as strictly as Islam. Thanks to this the pickaxe spared four beautiful baths built or reconstructed in the Turkish style in Buda in the second half of the sixteenth century. They still stand at the foot of Castle Hill, not far from the Danube. Two of them, the Király and Rudas baths, lend the city an Oriental character with their typical domes composed of spherical segments reminiscent of Turkish *djamis*. The other two, the Császár and Rácz, in use to this day, also preserved their dome-shaped roofs.

Another similar building with a characteristic dome recalling Turkish times in Buda is the *türbe* or funeral chapel of the dervish Gül Baba which stands on the Hill of Roses (Rózsadomb) north of Castle Hill. The crescent moon of the followers of the true faith of the Moslems glitters on its top even today.

Peace times, German times

After the expulsion of the Turks, a century and a half of peace descended on Pest-Buda, or shall we say Pest-Ofen. The latter name was more befitting in an age when the major-

231

ity of the inhabitants of both cities were German. Even the third community, Óbuda, or Alt-Ofen as it was known then, was occupied by them after the end of Turkish rule, when the Habsburg emperors residing in Vienna extended their power beyond Hungary, over the whole of the Carpathian Basin.

The emperors gave strict orders that only Germans, and Roman Catholic Germans at that, should be permitted to settle in the occupied towns.

Since the first half of the sixteenth century there were many Protestants—Lutherans and Calvinists—among the Hungarians. The number of "rebels", just as reluctant to bow to the Viennese Emperor as they had been to cringe before the Sultan of Istanbul, was considerable.

So settlers came to Buda, Óbuda and Pest and other Hungarian cities from the German Em-

233

232

232. *The Szarvas (Stag) House at the southern foot of Castle Hill*

234

235

236

233–234. *Houses in Ostrom Street, on the northern side of Castle Hill*
235. *Old house in Hunfalvy Street,*
236. *Old iron door-handle*
237. *The Lajos fountain on Corvin Square*
238. *Baroque statue of St. John of Nepomuk on the façade of the house No. 3 on Corvin Square*

pire. They were a mixed crowd of honest, decent tradesmen and craftsmen, but there were among them rather dubious elements as well.

The latter were numerous. In the newly established towns, the prisons were crammed; it took some time before the better-class of immigrants prevailed over the criminals and adventurers.

However, the buildings dating from these times show no trace of the chaos that reigned in the city, only that after lengthy struggle a period of lasting peace gradually set in. It was also a period of material growth, the building of the three cities on the Danube and the destruction of the Turkish *djamis* with their domes and slender minarets.

The style of the age was Baroque. It came to Hungary, too, although it did not reach the

237

238

239

territories under Turkish rule. Once the Turks had been driven out, the field was open to all ranks of masters of Baroque architecture. They left their mark on a large number of buildings both in Pest and Buda.

There were Italian and Hungarian architects among them; but most came from German territories. The effect was fruitful, just as fruitful as the Romanesque, Gothic or Renaissance styles had been at the times they became naturalized in architecture in Hungary.

The result was no doubt due partly to the large masses of German settlers, those who commissioned and those who executed the buildings.

Let us grant them their due. But at the same time, let us reject the contention that the backward barbarian Hungarians would not have been up to the task of creating an urban culture of any value without the help of the German settlers.

The kingdom, the power and the glory belonged to Vienna at that time. It was the Vienna of that period which decreed that the Hungarian citizenry was not to be allowed to grow too strong, least of all the citizens of the heart of the country, the two towns of Buda and Pest. In the eyes of the Hungarians, Vienna meant the Imperial Court. The Emperors there reigned over the land of Hungary as kings; but they neglected to make Budapest even their secondary seat, such as Prague became. For a long time, even the Royal Council of the Governor-General did not have its headquarters in Buda but in a western border town of Hungary, Pozsony (now Bratislava). Pest and Buda became provincial towns and life pro-

240

241

242

243

244

245 — 246

239–242. *St. Anne Church on Batthyány Square, one of the most beautiful Baroque monuments in Buda*
243. *The old terrace of the building on the corner of Fő and Pala Streets*
244. *Louis XVI style window in Szalag Street*
245. *Down in the distance Watertown, towards the sky, the Castle*
246. *The Rococo building of the former White Cross Inn on Batthyány Square*

ceeded there accordingly, far from Vienna, bathed in the brilliant light of imperial splendour.

However, a century later the offices of the Hungarian authorities moved to Buda. Certain restrictions had already been relaxed earlier: Hungarians had the right to settle, buy or build a house in Pest-Buda. Nevertheless, it took a long time before they outnumbered the Germans and a Hungarian Budapest was finally born.

Still, almost all the eighteenth century Baro-

247

248

249–250

247. *Statue of Eugene of Savoy (1663–1736) in front of the main façade of the Castle*
248. *Northern gate of the Castle's inner courtyard*
249. *The high cupola*

250. *The western wing is the new home of the National Library*
251. *A view of the inner courtyard*
252. *Ornamental fountain in front of the façade facing the Danube*
253–254. *The eastern wing of the Castle houses the National Gallery. The gallery of the cupola and the grand staircase*

que houses recall the early German small towns of Pest, Ofen and Alt-Ofen. The same applies to the Baroque churches and other contemporary buildings. The statue dedicated to the Holy Trinity, standing on Szentháromság Square in the heart of the Castle District, was also destined to protect the pious German population of the town against the raging plague of the time.
It was around this period that the building of the new Royal Palace was began. Not a single surviving wing of the ruined palace was

251

253

252

254

From the collection of the Hungarian National Gallery:
255. *Master of the St. Anne Altars (early 16th century): St. Anna Altar from Kisszeben (detail)*
256. *Master of Jánosrét (15th century): Main Altar of Jánosrét (detail)*
257. *Hungarian painter (15th century): The Madonna of Bártfa*

255

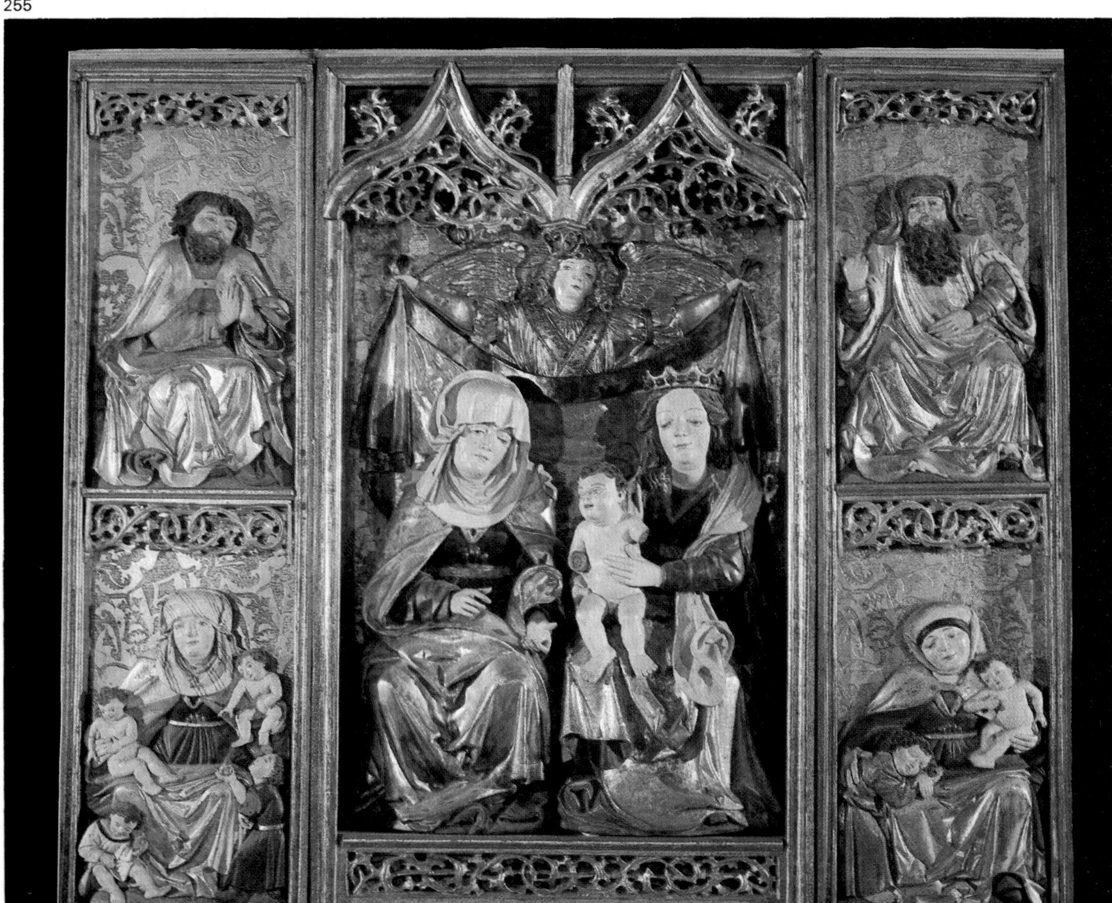

256

257

spared. The devastation caused by the Turks and the siege was completed by the pickaxe: King Matthias's once famous palace was literally razed to the ground. The stones and rubble were than levelled and the foundations of the new royal residence were built over them.

The new building was not planned to be either too large or too sumptuous, for the Habsburg rulers had not the slightest intention of moving from Vienna to Buda or even of spending a long period of time there.

When the palace was finished, the first wing was still very modest. Two further wings built in the Viennese Baroque style were added by Maria Theresa (1740–1780). The Baroque remained the dominant style also for the large-scale extension of the residence in the nineteenth century. However, no trace of it is extant today. After the siege of the Second World War, the huge building was restored in a much more puritan form. It now houses the National Széchényi Library, the Hungarian National Gallery, the Budapest Historical Museum, and other important cultural institutions.

A country in search of a heart

Vienna had never been accepted by Hungary as her "heart", for she never wanted to merge into the Habsburg Empire. Hungary wanted a destiny and a heart of her own. There was in this attitude a good deal of close-fistedness on the part of the Hungarian nobility. That of Austria and Bohemia had long lost its fiscal immunity, while Hungary still stood upon her ancient constitution and laws. In view of these circumstances, Maria Theresa decided to regulate the customs duties in a way that would make Hungary a safe market for Austrian and Bohemian industry and a steady supplier of cheap food and raw materials. Speaking of Hungary and Transylvania, one of her counsellors openly declared that he regarded these countries in the same light as the Indian colonies.

Prince Metternich, the great nineteenth century politician, was of the same opinion. "Hungary needs no industry," he declared, "every poor man there is needed for agricultural work."

However, the effects of this policy did not spare the German population either. It even made part of the Hungarian nobility partisans of civic progress in the country.

And so, the aggrieved parties found each other. Hungary began to feel that she did have a heart. It no longer mattered so much

258

258. *Mihály Munkácsy (1844–1900): Condemned Cell*
259. *József Rippl-Rónai (1861–1927): Woman with Cage*

260. *Lajos Gulácsy (1882–1932): The Magician's Garden*
261. *Béla Kondor (1931–1972): Christ I*

259

260

261

262. *Statue of poet Sándor Petőfi on the Danube embankment*
263. *The National Museum*

262

that the German settlers outnumbered the Hungarians in Pest-Buda.
From the first decades of the 1800s common endeavours became more and more marked. The nobility gradually realized that their close-fisted policy was not profitable. It was not worth while to be the privileged class of a backward country, the poor seigneurs of miserable serfs. General and proportionate sharing in taxation, freely flowing credit, freely circulating money, a developing industry, modern agriculture, the people of an independent country living and working for their own good, became the dominant aspirations of Hungary.
This exciting age left its mark on external aspects of the city as well. The features of Budapest—especially Pest—first of all on those of its building which were conceived in the Neo-Classical style.
Thus far, Buda had been in the lead over Pest. After all, it was there that the great kings of old had their seats, and the Turkish pashas ruled. The new Royal Palace of the Habsburgs was also built in Buda.
In the first half of the nineteenth century, however, Pest was being built up and generally developed. Trade on the Danube became more lively; the western provinces of the Em-

pire needed increasing quantities of Hungarian wheat, wine, wool, leather and other agricultural products which could be most conveniently transported over water. Due to the Napoleonic wars, oats and hay were also in great demand. The centre of exports of these from Hungary was Pest, and goods imported in exchange were also delivered here. The launching of public projects encouraged

264

265

266

267

268

From the collection of the National Museum:
264. *Scythian golden stag, 6th century B.C.*
265. *Title page of an illuminated manuscript from the Bibliotheca Corviniana*
266. *The Monomachos crown, 11th century*
267. *Lehel's horn, 9–10th century*
268. *Crown of St. Stephen, 11th century*
269. *Ornamental cup with lid, 1697*
270. *Miklós Barabás (1810–1898): Laying the Foundation Stone of the Chain Bridge*

269

wealthy middle-class citizens to invest their money. Three and four-storey houses and business establishments sprang up along the Danube and elsewhere within the city walls. In Buda, on the other hand, there was hardly any private building activity; it remained the small Baroque town it had been before, while Pest gradually grew into a large city dominated by the then fashionable Neo-Classical style.

Traces of these developments are still evident in Budapest, although hardly any of the Neo-Classical buildings of the age stand out conspicuously among the later eclectic ones.

One of the finest Neo-Classical historic monuments of the city is the edifice of the Hungarian National Museum with its flight of steps, colonnade and tympanum. It is a worthy spokesman for its times, the embodiment of respect for the past and hope for the future. It was built by the sons of a nation already aware of the fact that it was worth while to build a lasting home for the preservation of the country's historical relics and other public treasures.

There was never any uncertainty about the site of the building. It had to be erected in the heart of the country and in Pest, the city pervaded by the breath of the new times. Yet nobody suspected then that this beautiful new building was soon to become the scene of historic events. Nobody knew that from the base of the huge new columns, on the steps of the Museum, resounding revolutionary words would arouse the assembled masses on the morning of March 15, 1848, when Sándor Petőfi's famous poem "Talpra magyar" (Rise, Hungarians) first incited the nation to rebellion.

The movement for national revival, already many decades old, turned into a true revolution. The long period of slow, prudent progress was followed by one of radical reforms, rapid changes in society and eventually armed struggle for the independence of the country, lead by Lajos Kossuth. It was a

270

popular-national struggle and only the joint forces of two great powers—imperial Austria and czarist Russia—succeeded in suppressing it in blood in the late summer of 1849.

Years of labour

"The mind was aflame and the heart filled with hope." Hardly any other words could characterize better or more concisely the period preceding 1848. They were written by Mihály Vörösmarty who, after the defeat of the 1848–49 Hungarian War of Independence against the Habsburgs, became a persecuted refugee.

Pest and Buda, although not reduced to ashes, suffered a great deal from the cannons and siege during the war.

It looked then as if the country had no hope. The saying: *"finis Hungariae"* was no longer just a bad nightmare. The victorious powers divided Hungary into separate regions with local centres, all of which were controlled directly from Vienna.

Pest-Buda again ceased to be the heart of the country. But such complete numbness and hopelessness could not last long. Life did not come to an end. Industrious craftsmen continued their work, tradesmen their trade. At the beginning of 1848 the Hungarian nobility liberated their serfs, abolished their own exemption from taxation, and of their own accord introduced a general sharing of the public burdens. These measures survived the defeat of the revolution and proved favourable for the development of the bourgeoisie. This applied especially to Pest, which soon availed itself of the advantages of rail trans-

271

272

273

274

271–274. *The Vigadó (Municipal Concert Hall) of Pest built in the Romantic style, where Liszt, Wagner, Brahms and Mahler gave concerts*
275–276. *The Synagogue in Dohány Street*
277. *Rákóczi Road* — Looking West from Hársfa Utca. 2 blocks North of: Ferenc Körút / Lenin Körút

1854–1859

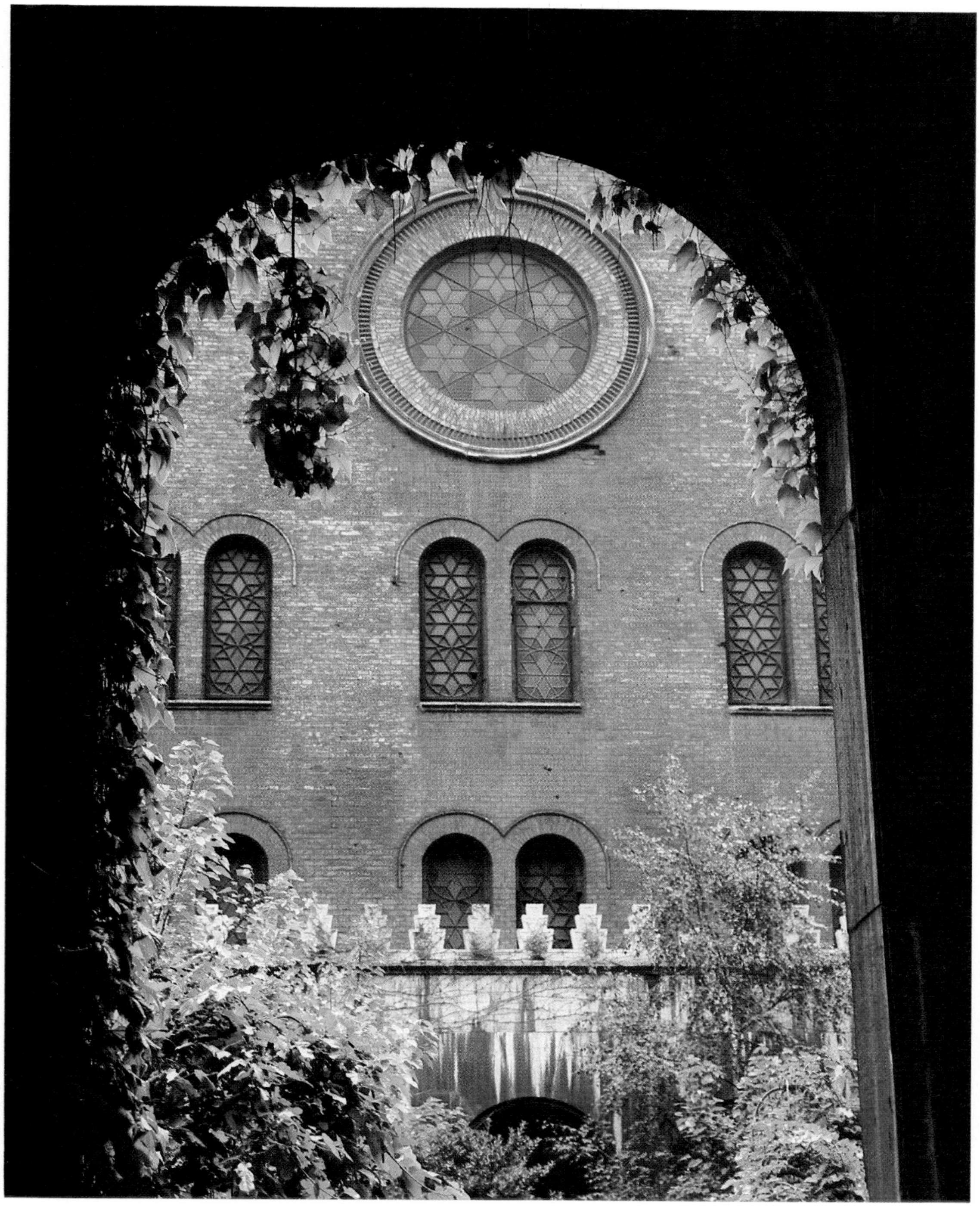

276

Palace Hotel on Left
Metropol " — Right
Erkel Theatre on Left. Largest in Hungary

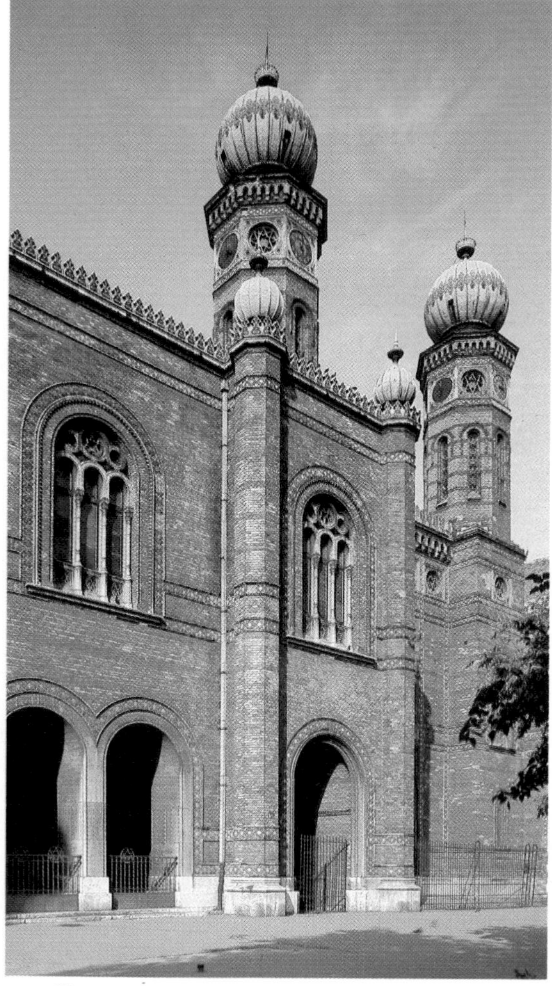

port in addition to the shipping on the Danube. Where money circulates, people cease to brood over the past. Not only tombstones were set up; houses were built too.

The architecture of the age was characterized by the late-Romantic style. The buildings then created were all individualistic. Most important were the Hungarian Academy of Sciences, the Vigadó (Municipal Concert Hall) where Liszt and Brahms gave recitals, and the Synagogue of Pest in Dohány utca. The latter points to the increasing role played by the Jews in Hungary's economic life. The revolution of 1848 achieved for them a comparative equality of rights and the possibility of free enterprise. They had a stake in preserving Pest-Buda as the heart of the country even when it did not exist officially. These were no easy times. Tears mingled with blood while they lasted. However, in 1867, after long procrastination, Francis Joseph and the liberal Hungarian politicians came to a compromise. Long-drawn-out negotiations resulted in the birth of a dual monarchy, two co-dominions with equal rights and separate parliaments; two reponsible governments but one Francis Joseph who, although he continued to act as Emperor in Vienna, was only regarded as King of Hungary by the population of Budapest.

SZÍNHÁZ
PALACE
SZALON
ÁRUHÁZ
PEPSI

TAKARÉK
PÉNZTÁR
RUGALMAS
PEPSI
HOTEL
HOTEL
HÁRSFA UTCA

The birth of a metropolis

In the ancient coat of arms of the Habsburg dynasty, a double-eagle spreads its black wings. In 1867, the Habsburg Empire also became double-headed, with one head in Vienna, the other in Budapest.

Vienna had grown into a large city a long time before; but in comparison, Budapest was still somewhat undeveloped. It was time to catch up with Vienna, not only in size, but also in beauty, not just in the number of stones, but also in the quality of cultural life. Modern town-planning began. Boulevards and avenues were built. Strict building regulations directed development into the desired channels. A city-wide water-, sewage- and gas-system were developed, and public lighting and solid pavements formed part of the new projects. Bridges were constructed over the Danube. The city was enriched with new theatres and an Academy of Music that rivalled the one in Vienna; an Opera House, picture galleries, museums, exhibition halls and a Polytechnic were also built. The huge Parliament Building, the Stock Exchange and a series of other public buildings were among the newly erected establishments.

European architecture was dominated by the Eclectic style. This meant a practically unlimited mixture of styles, a little of this, and a little of that. The buildings of the age showed a combination of details that would hitherto have been regarded as incongruous. Romanesque, Gothic, Renaissance, Baroque, Neo-Classical and even romanticized elements appeared side by side. Now one was emphasized, now an other, often with the ostentatiousness of the newly rich.

Indeed, the greater part of Budapest was at that time the city of the newly rich. The members of the thriving bourgeoisie—whether of German, Jewish or some other origin—proved to be enthusiastic Hungarian patriots. Equality of rank for Hungary within the Habsburg monarchy was propitious in no small way for the Hungarian capitalist investors. This applied to the whole country, but in particular to Budapest. The rapidly developing railway network converging on Budapest brought most raw materials here for processing, and excess rural manpower was also absorbed by the capital. On the outskirts of the city and even within its boundaries a

278–279. *Newly painted Eclectic mansions along the Great Boulevard and Museum Boulevard*

280

280. *The silent statues of the Basilica and the bustling city*
282–283. *Bajcsy-Zsilinszky Road: Eclecticism and Art Nouveau*
281., 284. *Two gates and two styles on Szent István Boulevard*

282

283

variety of new factories were built, accompanied by overcrowded apartment houses for the workers flocking to Budapest. This had, above all, an animating effect on inner Budapest which grew in size as well as in wealth. The beauty of the eclectic apartment houses masked as palaces has since worn off. Good style in architecture mellows with age; what is merely showy later causes disappointment. The question arises as to what happens when such buildings get restored, repainted or rejuvenated in some other way?
In Pest—which is a truly eclectic city—there have recently been attempts to do this by giving some of the main thoroughfares a face-lift. The experiment was not without success. The freshly painted houses have lost their hundred-year-old tiresomely dull aspect and —as if by some miracle—have become res-

281

284

285

286

287

285. *Rooftops of the Inner City*
286. *Szent István Boulevard* ✓
287. *19th-century ornamentation on a façade*

✓ Looking East to Marx Square

288

289

290

291

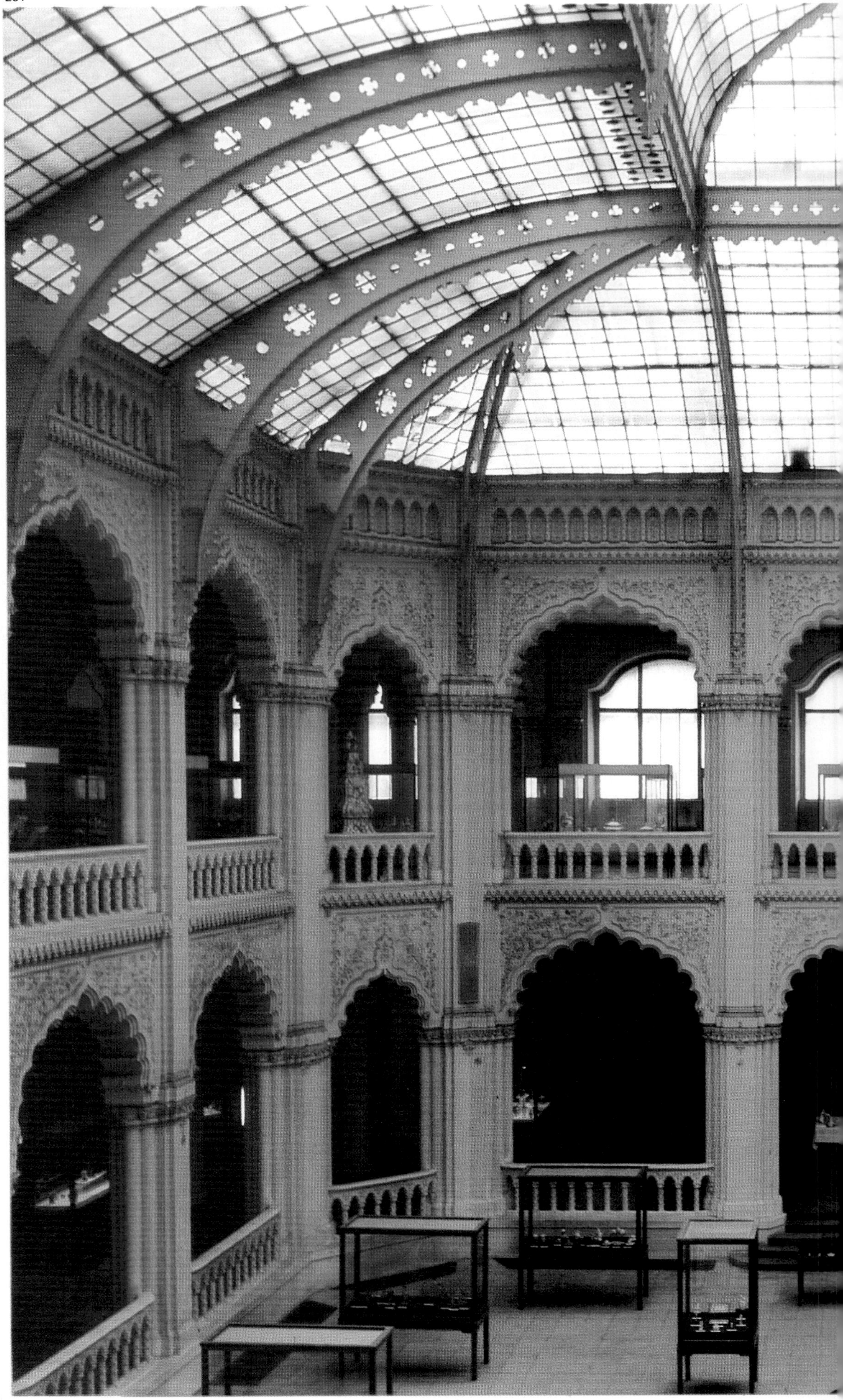

plendent again. The question remains: for how long?
It is evident, however, that the values that the Eclectic buildings represent in Pest, the beauty that in the great palace-like apartment houses have been preserved, are worthy of consideration, the more so because the public buildings of the city followed this style from the building of Parliament to the Opera House, from the Cathedral to the Budapest Library, from the Neo-Romanesque Fishermen's Bastion to the Neo-Romanesque-Neo-Gothic-Neo-Renaissance-Neo-Baroque building complex in City Park.
But is it beautiful? Let the question go unchallenged. It is interesting, no doubt about that; as interesting as the whole of one-time Budapest which vied with Vienna and developed feverishly in its striving to become a real metropolis.

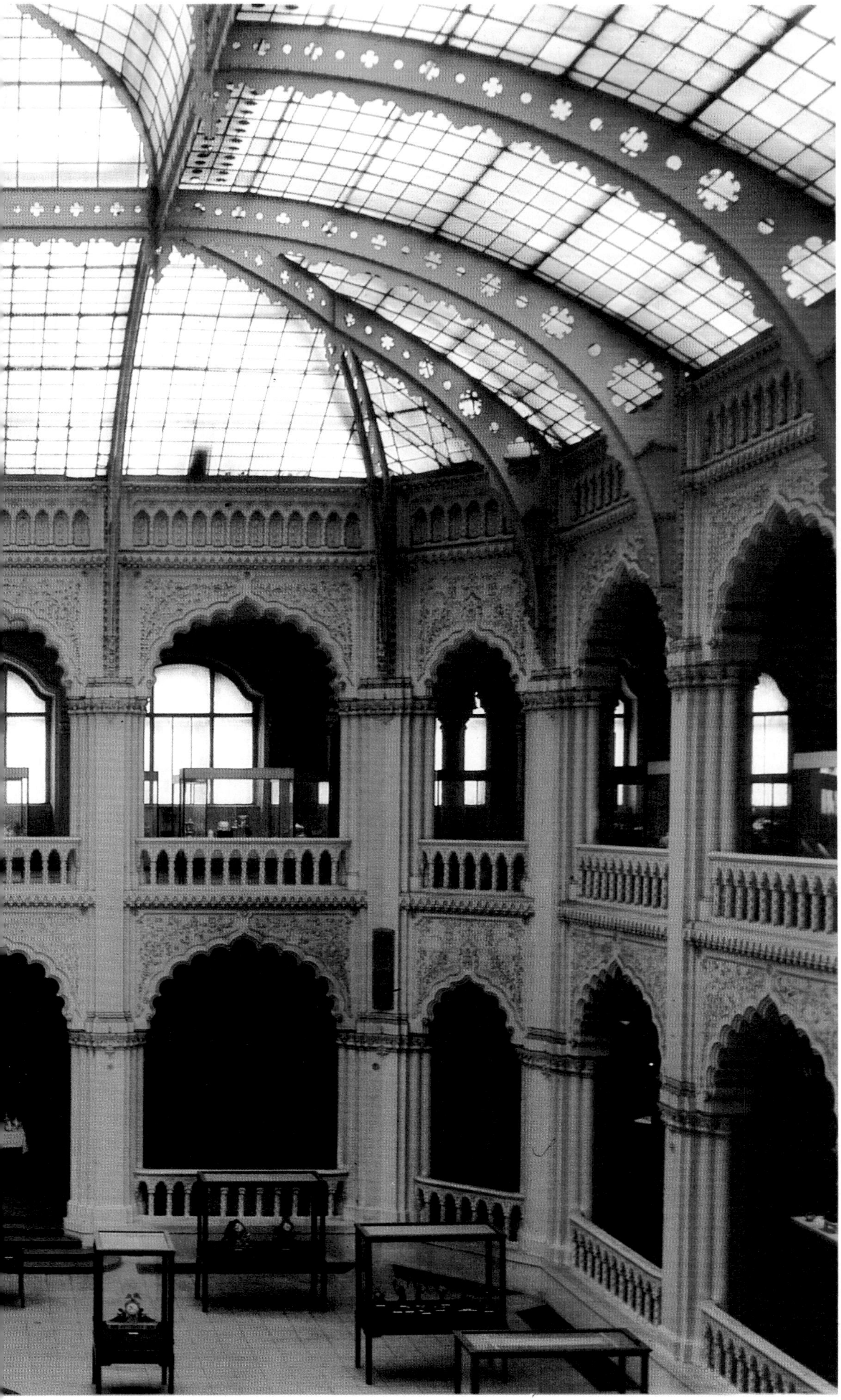

1893–6

291. *The main hall of the Museum of Applied Arts* IX, 33-37 Üllői út

Iparművészeti Múzeum

292

293

294

(1)

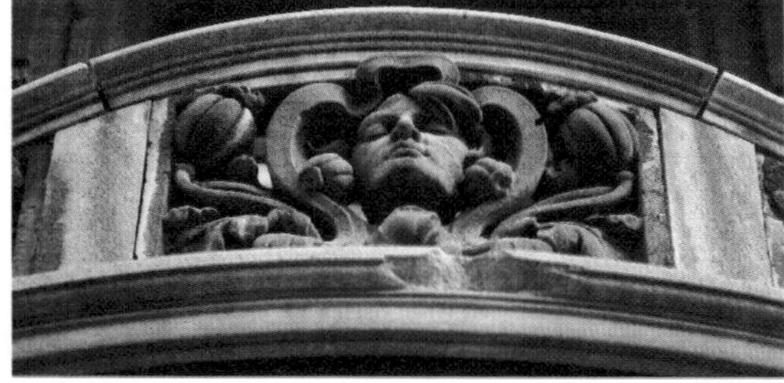

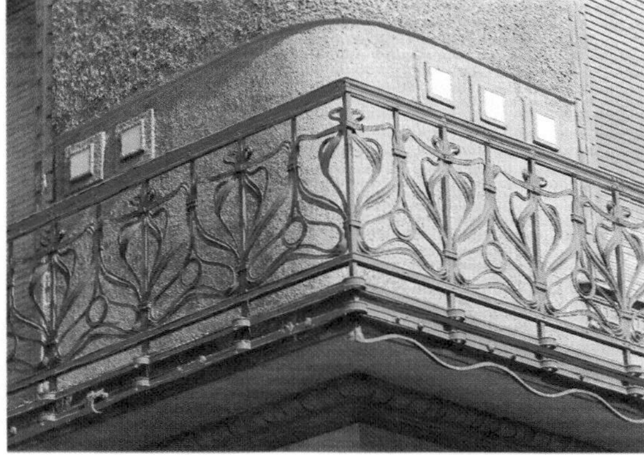

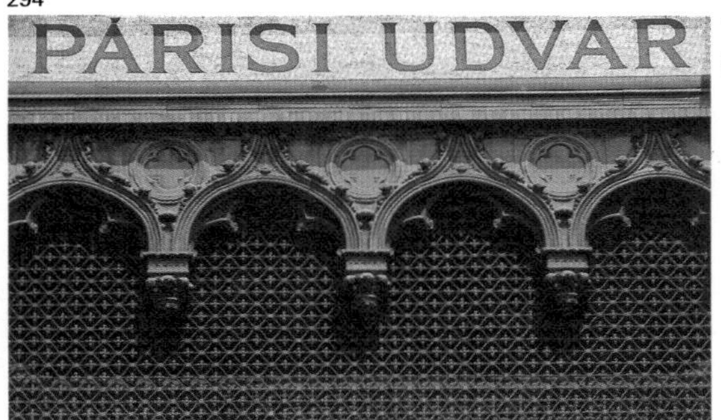

The troubled beginning of the new century

At the end of the last century the city grew and developed rapidly, but not restlessly. Then, a certain strange restlessness set in. There was something in the air that made itself felt not only in Budapest, but throughout Europe. Was it the smell of gunpowder? The premonitory sign of a cruel war, or of an all subverting revolution? Nobody reckoned with a cataclysm like the one that affected the world in 1914, though people did expect some menacing change.

At the beginning of the century, the Hungarian capital was already one of the important centres of the artistic endeavours which arose from this restless, foreboding outlook. It is perhaps sufficient to mention the names of Csontváry, the painter, Béla Bartók and

(1) Runs East from Váci utca through Petőfi Sándor utca

295. *The Art Noveau period between the two world wars in architecture: what is not functional can't be beautiful (Houses on Madách Square)*

296. *The blending of the centuries in Óbuda*

295

Zoltán Kodály, the composers, György Lukács, the philosopher, and Endre Ady, the poet.

Budapest had no architect of such stature. But it did have some who were capable of perpetuating in their buildings the restless modern spirit, the negation of past, and the search for new ways of expression which prevailed here in the early part of the century. They were the architects who created the Hungarian version of the European Art Nouveau.

They were extreme individualists, like all artists who followed this new trend in the arts. So they never developed a common style. Yet their works embodied the same spirit of the age; an age that no longer knew whether it could believe in itself, and this very doubt made it bold. Its boldness developed under the pressure of circumstance. It was mocked and even held in contempt by modern architecture, though the latter only took wing before the First World War and gained ground repeatedly after it. We now hold it again in higher esteem, and do not believe in discarding everything that architecture has achieved by a rejection of earlier combinations of colours, lines, planes and space.

Between the two world wars

At the end of the First World War the Habsburg monarchy collapsed. The states of the Carpathian Basin, including thousand-year-old historic Hungary, fell to pieces. Since 1867, Budapest had been the capital of the eastern half of a European Great Power, the centre of a territory of 300 thousand square kilometres. Of this, only 93,000 remained.

Vienna suffered the same fate. But neither city diminished in size on that account. On the contrary, they became comparatively larger. In such cases the law according to which disproportionately large cities absorb everything, concentrating in themselves all the energy destined to promote development, is fulfilled. Being already too large, cities continue to grow, although this is no longer good for them.

Half of the country's industry was concentrated in Budapest and its surroundings. First one-sixth, later one-fifth of the population came to live here. Among all the European countries, only Austria had such a disproportionately large capital at that time. The much talked of predominance of Paris over the provincial towns of France did not even approach the relationship of Budapest

or Vienna to the provincial communities of their respective countries.

Budapest is just as centrally situated as Paris; it forms the junction of a star-shaped road and railroad network. No excuses were offered; the Hungarian capital had to develop further. It had to swell, grow, become built up, even if at a slower pace than before, and even at the cost of leaving other parts of the country comparatively undeveloped.

By this time the architects cursed Art Nouveau. Rational, simple, yet aesthetic three-dimensional forms were now being adopted in Budapest. Elements devoid of function were barely tolerated, on the grounds that what is not functional cannot be beautiful.

Although a new style set in, it left few marks on the architecture of the 1920s and 30s. This was partly due to the impoverished state of the country. Moreover, the years of construction were very soon followed by the devastation of yet another war.

The present and the future

After the Second World War most of Budapest lay in ruins. However, the 1944–45 devastation of the city did more than merely cause distress, it raised hopes, too. For it was to be followed by the advent of a great new epoch. The people of Budapest, liberated at last from Hitlerian domination believed and hoped that all the old evils could be made good. All they had to do was to bury the past and accept the promise of a better future.

All at once, everything was in ferment. Daring new ideas were born in the field of

297

town-planning. Outstanding architects thought the time ripe, for instance, for opening green corridors in the densely built districts of Pest, to allow open passage to the fresh air flowing almost continuously from the forests of the Danube Bend. However, this dream soon vanished when the housing shortage caused the shelving of every such town-planning idea.

For obvious reasons, only those houses were demolished after the war which had been so severely damaged as to be absolutely uninhabitable and whose restoration was quite hopeless. Even so, the streets were studded with vacant lots. Gradually most of these were built up. To link such lots into a green corridor would have required the sacrificing of whole blocks of crowded town dwellings, and the moving of the people living in them elsewhere. But where?

This "where" has remained a vital problem up to the present day. In the meantime, the demolition of damaged older houses has become ever more urgent in the densely built inner districts of Pest. People crammed into the "belly" of the city have a craving for more space, larger grassy expanses, more trees, air and sunlight.

In the past decades, new housing estates have increased the number of dwellings in Budapest by hundreds of thousands; yet even so, shortages still exist. True, some of the housing estates necessitated first making a clean sweep of existing old buildings. In Óbuda, for example, whole rows of old one-story houses had to be levelled.

On the outskirts it was easy to demolish structures, but in the inner part of Pest it is still impossible, even today.

This may, however, be a fortunate circumstance. The decades of delay brought about something good; for besides the further aging and decay of the century-old public housing units, there has grown up an ever increasing attachment to *historic* Pest.

The antique stones of Buda carry with them a 700-year-old history, while the ruins of Óbuda have a history of nearly two millenia. Pest can boast no such antiquity. It lacks, above all, anything similar to the Castle District blessed with so many ancient remains rising above the more recently developed parts of the city.

Apart from a number of scattered Baroque, Neo-Classical and Romanticized buildings, inner Pest is dominated first of all by the Eclectic and Art Nouveau that has survived from the turn of the century. This gives it a

298

299

297–299. *It would be a shame to destroy everything that is worn or old...*

300

300–303. *The too rational lines of the new buildings only enhance our nostalgia for the more personal beauty of bygone times*

303

301

302

historic atmosphere, and as the years go by, will make the city even more interesting and valuable, especially in the face of the growing number of bleak panel houses in the new housing estates. It is clear by now that the Inner City on the left bank of the Danube must be renovated and opened up with all due consideration to its heritage. While green areas must be provided, the notable creations of modern architecture, together with the whole pre-First World War aspect of the city, that "newly rich" inner part of Pest which grew so eagerly in the old days, must be revived and preserved.

On the old outskirts, most of which became attached to Budapest in 1949, the situation is different. In these areas there are hardly any remains worth preserving, and architects can have a free hand. They must bring the housing projects to a successful conclusion, building flats by the thousands and ten thousands, as well as stores, libraries, schools, sports grounds and others establishments without which a modern housing estate cannot exist. Historic Pest and Buda remain the main centres of the capital. It is proposed, however, to make the surrounding sub-centres grow as attractively as possible, particularly as de-

304

306

veloping cultural centres. For it must be born in mind that new homes may facilitate, but cannot in themselves bring to fullness the lives of people in the multi-storied standardized buildings of the new housing estates. It is imperative that they be less dull, less monotonous. Today, everyone is painfully aware of the rapidly rising demand for just this.

The town-planners of Budapest must also reckon with this demand. A rational order of forms and colours is important. Important, yes, but not sufficient. Man is not only a rational being. He also has a soul, sentiments, attachments and a constant desire for something new. That this has been recognized, appears from the articulated forms and lively colours of schools in the new housing estates. There are many individually designed buildings, generally surrounded by carefully tended parks. The urge towards the humanizing of the environment also shows up in the many new statues, monuments and fountains set up in public squares, and even in the growing appreciation for historic districts and especially for Art Nouveau decoration.

305

307

The inhabitants of the city

Who live in Budapest?

Many kinds of people throng the main streets and thoroughfares of the city. One hears different languages spoken. However, those speaking a language other than Hungarian are almost certain to be tourists, businessmen, specialists, reporters, delegates, foreign students studying in Budapest, etc.—People who happen to be here now but will leave soon.

Almost all those who settle here come from different regions of Hungary. They make up for the lack of increase in the population which typifies most large cities.

In most economically-advanced countries, the only reason why the population of big cities does not diminish rapidly is because there are continuous replacements coming from smaller settlements. This applies also to Budapest.

A few decades ago, there were so many people moving into the capital that the number of its inhabitants grew rapidly. It reached and even exceeded the two million figure; but then the increase stopped, and more recently, a slow decrease has set in. As it is well known, this is always incidental to a certain process of ageing. But for the time being, this hardly shows in the life of the city. Whichever part of the world people come from, when they are

308

310

309

311

LGT

314

confronted by the day-to-day life of Pest and Buda, they see that this Central European metropolis is inhabited by a very energetic people.

This is, of course, partly due to the fact that Budapest, with its two million inhabitants, attracts almost every important organization to itself from the whole of Hungary. Here we find the largest scientific institutions, research centres, libraries, archives, museums, theatres and orchestras; the only Hungarian film studios, the national radio and television headquarters; it is here that the most outstanding artists and writers work, most university and college students study; ministries and other national institutions function along with industrial and trading enterprises, banks, and insurance companies. All this gives the city an advantage over others within the country, and contributes to its undisputed dynamism. But Budapest owes its vitality also to the openness without which no small country can hold its own any longer in the world. Although its main virtue lies in the fact that it is the queen of Hungarian cities; its inhabitants are well aware that this superiority is but relative, that they must watch the people in other countries, learn and get information from them, take part in the international exchange of material and intellectual life and in the obstinate rat race of these days, in a way that even in critical circumstances will not make Hungarians the losers. Budapest is today one of the most sober metropolises of Europe. It aspires to neither more nor less than it is capable of. It indulges but little in fancies or reveries; instead, it perseveres in its search for realistic approaches to the future.

Budapest is neither young nor old; its situation has not predestined it for either. It may yet see difficult times, but its sources of strength are inexhaustible; as long as people continue to live here, it will always be reborn. The present-day inhabitants of Budapest soberly reckon with their circumstances. They recall the fate of two thousand-year-old Aquincum, one thousand-year-old Pest-Buda, the ruined city of the winter of 1944–1945, and they do not doubt that Budapest will always survive and find new possibilities for prospering.

Today this matter of survival and prosperity is in their own hands. They work for it, and their labour is evident on the face of the city. However, the result of earlier labours, those of their ancestors, Hungarians and non-Hungarians alike, some known by name and others unsung, are also there. These forefathers deserve our love and gratitude for what Budapest is today.

304–314. *It's not a new city, but nor is it old*

	The photographs were taken by:
Imre Benkő	43
Lóránt Bérczi	12, 50, 140, 141, 146, 156, 172, 221, 226, 230, 252, 291
Lajos Czeizing	36, 38, 114, 116, 117, 132, 225
Sándor Cs. Kovács	277
László Csigó	17, 18, 34, 49, 50, 62, 295
Tamás Diener	25, 26, 27, 28, 76, 77, 92, 93, 102, 104, 105, 118, 187, 189, 196, 198, 203
János Eifert	95, 97, 98, 99, 103, 106, 107, 113, 115, 117, 120, 121, 124, 247, 248, 251, 254, 301, 302
István Faragó	15, 22, 65, 67, 179, 188, 197, 207, 209, 240, 283, 285, 287, 288, 289, 290, 292, 293, 294, 299, 313
Ernő Fejér	55, 192
György Gara	6, 11, 16, 24, 31, 52, 53, 56, 57, 59, 94, 139, 144, 145, 148, 161, 163, 164, 175, 176, 182, 183, 185, 191, 193, 200, 201, 202, 204, 205, 210, 211, 212, 215, 217, 218, 219, 220, 222, 233, 234, 235, 236, 237, 238, 239, 241, 242, 243, 244, 249, 250, 281, 284
László Gyarmathy	4, 41, 47, 48, 73, 138, 147, 157, 158, 271
András Hász	64, 100, 135, 136, 137, 276
György Hegedüs	312
Károly Hemző	3, 5, 20, 29, 91, 101, 109, 119, 123, 134, 162, 213, 224, 229, 231, 262, 275, 307
János Huschit	70, 282, 296
Károly Kastaly	160, 206, 300
György Kapocsy	96
Péter Kornis	7, 23, 88, 89, 90, 131, 143, 208, 246
Albert Kozák	(MTI) 155, 159, 253
Lajos Köteles	194, 199, 232
Endre Lábas	69, 133
Árpád Patyi	227
Endre Rácz	112, 142, 151, 153, 297, 298, 304
Csaba Ráffael	(MTI) Jacket, 274
Tamás Révész	35, 54, 110, 111, 228
Herbert Saphier	263
Béla Schichmann	(MTI) 154
Péter Siklós	68
József Szabó	9
Zsolt Szabóky	1, 2, 10, 13, 14, 19, 21, 32, 39, 40, 42, 44, 58, 66, 71, 74, 75, 122, 124, 126, 127, 128, 129, 130, 149, 150, 152, 171, 174, 177, 178, 180, 181, 223, 245, 272, 278, 280, 286, 305, 306, 309, 310, 311
Zoltán Szalai	273
Károly Szelényi	8, 45, 82, 125, 165, 167, 169, 170, 216, 264, 265, 266, 268, 269
János Szerencsés	37, 72, 186, 267
Alfréd Schiller	78, 79, 80, 81, 83, 84, 85, 86, 87, 255, 256, 257, 270
Gyula Tahin	63, 108, 173, 195, 279, 303
Bence Tihanyi	166, 168
András Tokaji	30, 33, 46, 51, 60, 184;
István Vidovics	314

READ 91 JUL 26

EDWARD HAMILTON, BOOKS
FALLS VILLAGE, CONN.
R– 91 JUL 24

14.95 [LIST – 27.50]
1.50 – PR–SH ½
1.31 ~~PR~~ – ST
$17.76